LIVING WITH OUR DEAD

Delphine Horvilleur

LIVING WITH OUR DEAD

ON LOSS AND CONSOLATION

*Translated from the French
by Lisa Appignanesi*

Europa
editions

Europa Editions
27 Union Square West, Suite 302
New York NY 10003
www.europaeditions.com
info@europaeditions.com

Library of Congress Cataloging in Publication Data is available
ISBN 978-1-60945-795-2

Horvilleur, Delphine
Living with Our Dead

Cover image and design by Ginevra Rapisardi

Prepress by Grafica Punto Print—Rome

Printed in Canada

CONTENTS

In memory of my grandfather, Nathan Horvilleur

And for Samuel, Ella, and Alma,
who always bring me back to life.

I have put before you life and death,
blessing and curse. Choose life . . .
—DEUTERONOMY 30:19

Life is the totality of functions capable of utilizing death.
—HENRI ATLAN

Essentially, if death didn't exist,
life would lose its comic aspect.
—ROMAIN GARY

LIVING WITH
OUR DEAD

Azrael

Life and Death in One Hand

I t seems inevitable. No sooner am I in the cemetery and about to start conducting a funeral service than my phone rings.

"I can't talk right now," I murmur. "I'll call back after the burial."

This scene is so often repeated that my friends now make a mockery of it. When they call me, they begin by joking, "So who died today?" or "How's life going in the cemetery?" My frequent visits to a place where others rarely or never go make me a regular subject of interrogation. "Doesn't it bother you to live so close to death? Isn't it hard being so often around people who are in mourning?"

For years now, I've been ducking the subject by providing random answers:

"No, no, you get used to it."

"Yes, yes, it's awful, and repetition doesn't make it any easier."

"In fact, it all depends on the day or the situation."

"Good question, thanks for raising it."

To tell the truth, I don't have an adequate response. I don't know what effect death really has on those who are nearing the end or on their loved ones. Nor am I capable of assessing death's influence on me, since I don't know what kind of woman I would have been had I taken care to distance myself from it.

What I do know is that over time I've adopted rituals or

habits some would call superstitious and others obsessive-compulsive. In a somewhat arbitrary way, they help me to limit death's place in my life.

I never go straight home from the cemetery. After a funeral, I make a detour to a café or shop—it doesn't matter which. I create a symbolic airlock between death and my house. Out of the question to bring death home. Whatever the cost, I have to scatter its force, leave it elsewhere—beside a cup of coffee, or in a museum or a changing room—to reassure myself that it's lost my scent and, above all, won't find out where I live.

In Jewish tradition, a thousand tales recount that death can follow you but that there are ways of warding it off and arranging things so it can't track you down. Numerous legends describe death in the guise of an angel who walks through our towns and visits our houses.

This angel even has a name—Azrael, the angel of death. Sword in hand, the stories say, he lurks in the vicinity of those he intends to strike. The tales may be fantastical, but they lead to inventive practices. In many Jewish families, when someone falls ill, their first name is changed. The idea is to confuse that supernatural being who's had the awful idea of coming for them. Imagine: the angel of death rings your doorbell in search of the life of a certain Moses. You can now easily reply, "So sorry, nobody by the name of Moses lives here. You're at Solomon's house." And the sheepish angel must apologize for having troubled you, turn around, and go away.

This stratagem might make you laugh, but it proffers a subtle truth. Part of being human is to believe that you can keep death at a distance. You can create barriers, stories, schemes to hold it at bay, or persuade yourself that rituals or words can confer this power on you.

Modernity, with its medicine and technology, has developed its own methods. These days the angel of death is kept far from our homes. He is invited to show himself only in hospitals, clinics, nursing homes, and hospices, preferably at times when they're closed to the public. Fewer and fewer people die at home, as if to protect the living from a suffering that has no connection to their lives. We prefer to think death has nothing to do with us.

I often think of this separation of spaces when I walk through Paris and discover historic plaques on the facades of old buildings. Here, so-and-so died; there, such-and-such celebrity passed away. As for the rest of us, we rarely even seem to know if anyone is dying in our own building. We're careful to avoid thinking of all those who may well have met their end in the very rooms we inhabit. Death has its domains clearly marked out. By delimiting its territory, we think we can constrain it to its own haunts.

But sometimes history, with its unpredictable turns, reminds us that our power is limited, despite all our ruses and tales.

In 2020, across the world, the angel of death decided to visit almost everywhere, knocking at doors on each continent. As I write these lines, he does not seem altogether ready to be driven away. Death certainly still prefers to strike Covid patients in hospitals and emergency wards, far from our homes, yet the pandemic is a reminder that death has the power to meddle in all our lives. The fear that it might infiltrate our territory, or take a family member, is palpable. The angel we hoped to keep at a distance now demands that we make space for him in our lives and societies. He knows our name, our address, and he won't easily be tricked.

The pandemic has also transformed both funeral rites and the expectations of mourners. Like all those who accompany the dying, over these last months and years I have witnessed situations I could not have imagined before.

Bedside visits when our masks and gloves deprived the

dying of a smile or an outstretched hand; isolation enforced on the elderly to protect them from a death which would find them anyway but would find them desperately alone; closed funerals in which the number of mourners was strictly counted, where hugs or handshakes were forbidden. We had to endure this and tell ourselves we would reflect on all of it later. Too late.

One day, at the very start of the first lockdown, a family called me from the cemetery. They were alone with their father's coffin, without anyone at their side. They had asked no friend to accompany them: they didn't want to endanger anyone. But they didn't know a single Jewish prayer, and they begged me to help them from a distance. So, I whispered words into their ears, which they repeated aloud. For the first time in my life, I led a burial service from the living room of my apartment, for a family I had never seen. When I hung up, I told myself that the old separation between life and death was now gone. Without any authorization, death had entered the places belonging to our everyday lives.

It had found our addresses and stolen into our homes, into our families or our consciousness. Death was reminding us that it had never really gone away, that it had assumed its rightful place, that our own power lay merely in choosing the words and gestures we would pronounce at the moment it chose to show itself.

Finding the words and knowing the gestures is at the heart of my work. For years now, I've been trying to define the nature of that work for those who ask it of me.

What does it mean to be a rabbi? Of course, it entails officiating, accompanying, teaching. It means translating texts, having them read so that each new generation can hear the voice of a tradition that awaits them to transmit it in turn. Yet as the years go by, it increasingly seems to me that the profession closest to mine has a name: storyteller.

Knowing how to narrate what has been said a thousand times before, while giving the person who hears the story for the first time unique keys with which to unlock the meaning for themselves—that is my function. I stand by the side of women and men who, at turning points in their lives, need stories. These ancestral stories are not only Jewish, but I speak them in the language of this tradition. They create bridges between eras and generations, between those who were and those who will be. These sacred stories open a path between the living and the dead. The role of a storyteller is to stand by the gate to ensure that it stays open.

And so, the question of space and separation rests with us. We like to think that the walls are impenetrable, that life and death are hermetically separated, and that the living and the dead need never cross paths. But what if, in reality, that's all they ever do?

I remember the first time I saw a dead person. It was in Jerusalem, and she was a woman. I was then a medical student, and that semester was devoted to anatomy. After the theoretical work, we were meant to spend several weeks on dissection. Each one of us was assigned a workstation, in other words a table on which lay a person who had donated their body to science. The heady odor of formalin comes back to me. It impregnated the bodies we were examining—organ by organ, muscle by muscle, nerve by nerve.

Probably to protect ourselves emotionally, to distance fear and apprehension, we stopped seeing these cadavers as single organisms. Instead, we focused on each anatomical part separately, disconnecting one from the other. The challenge was to reassure ourselves, as efficiently as possible, that every element conformed to the details in the textbook we had meticulously memorized.

One day we had to study the anatomy of the hand and ensure that we could recognize each of the ligaments, distinguish the artery and the ulnar nerve, the cubital vein and the flexor muscle. On lifting the sheet draped over the right arm of the cadaver I had been dissecting for several days now, I felt a wave of nausea. At the very tip of the hand of this woman who had donated her body to science, the well-filed nails—which had undoubtedly grown since her death—were covered in an elegant pink polish.

She had probably applied it very soon before her death. You could imagine that the final layer had barely had time to dry when Azrael knocked at her door, sword in hand, to end the life of this woman whose hand was so prettily manicured. The vision overwhelmed me. I felt as if an unspeakable reality had confronted me, an obvious fact that we medical students refused to articulate: each of the cadavers we dissected told the story of a man or a woman, of an undoubtedly complex and tormented life made up of depths and superficialities, made up, too, of the decisions—possibly formulated on one and the same day—to contribute to the advancement of science and to paint one's nails.

In that anatomy room at the medical school, life and death met at the fingertips of a woman whom I now saw differently. One of the more famous truisms leapt into my mind, a commonplace that for me contains the greatest wisdom ever pronounced: "Five minutes before dying, she was still alive."

To say this, even if it's a statement of the obvious, is to recognize that until the last second, even when death is inevitable, life doesn't allow itself to be completely taken away. Life makes its presence felt in the very moment that precedes our dying and until the end seems to be saying to death that there is a way of coexisting.

Perhaps this cohabitation doesn't in fact need to wait for death. Throughout our existence, without our being aware of it, life and death continually hold hands and dance.

Their closeness came to me in a book dating from those same years in medical school. In a slightly troubling fashion, I was again focusing in on the hand and its biology. In my embryogenesis courses during which we studied the stages in the formation of life *in utero*, I had discovered that, like many of the organs in our body, our fingers are formed through cellular death. Our hand first develops in the shape of a palm—a single entity with no spaces between its extremities. It's only later that, in the normal process of evolution, the fingers grow individualized and separate one by one through a destruction of the cells which initially joined them to each other. To put this another way, our bodies are sculpted by the death of the very elements that composed them. This is the case not only for each of our digital extremities, but also for many of the cavities in our organism: heart, intestines, nervous system. They can only fulfil their functions once an empty space has been excavated within them. It's the very disappearance of a part of them which allows these organs to work. It seems we owe life to the death which has taken place in its making.

This phenomenon of death lying at the heart of life has been studied by a researcher and peerless storyteller, Jean-Claude Ameisen, who was fascinated by the process of apoptosis, a form of programmed cell death. The word comes from Greek and literally means "a falling off," in reference to autumnal trees losing their leaves.

The seasons of existence both for trees and humans mean that life can only continue if visited by death. Spring only comes for those who undergo apoptosis and allow death to sculpt the possibility of a renaissance. Cancer research today tells us a similar tale: cells which surge with life, near-immortal cells which refuse to die, turn into tumors. Their excess of life condemns us: the very fact that their death has been inhibited is fatal to us. It's when life and death hold hands that history can go on.

I studied anatomy, biology, embryogenesis, but I didn't become a doctor or a researcher. I ultimately chose to accompany the living in another way.

In my profession as rabbi, it seems to me that what I learned from biology and the life sciences finds other translations. My knowledge of the body enters into a dialogue with the narratives I now hold in me.

Biology taught me the extent to which death is part of our lives. My rabbinical work gives me daily lessons in how we can make the inverse just as true: in death a place can be left for the living. For that to happen, we need to be able to tell their stories, find the words which will preserve them more powerfully than formalin. Each time I conduct a burial at the cemetery, I try to pay homage to that place and to augment it through the power of stories that leave indelible traces in us, that offer a prolongation of the dead within the living.

The book you now hold in your hands brings together several stories that I have been given to tell, of lives and of periods of mourning that I have lived through or witnessed. In some, details have been changed in order to respect fully the privacy of the bereaved. Others are completely faithful to reality and have been written with the agreement of the families concerned.

To all those men and women at whose sides I stood and whose stories do or do not figure in these pages, I address my infinite gratitude and underscore what an honor it was to be with them, hand in hand.

ELSA

In the House of the Living

So, tell me . . . "
She started each of her sessions with these words. She invited her patients to approach analysis in the same way they might pick up the thread of a story. Elsa Cayat loved stories. She knew how to tell them, write them, and listen to them.

She never had a chance to hear this one, which begins soon after her death. I would so love to tell her the story of her afterlife, tell her where our grief took us, and imagine the analysis she would have made of this disjointed narrative.

It's Thursday, January 15, 2015. It's noon, and there's already an immense crowd waiting at the gates of Montparnasse Cemetery. But there's hardly a sound. Our strangled voices stand in for the muteness of an entire nation. For eight days now, no one has been able to find adequate words.

Last Wednesday, a burst of shots ruptured time and froze memory. Everyone remembers exactly where they were when the news came of the massacre at the satirical magazine *Charlie Hebdo*, remembers the conversation they were having when death interrupted.

In a few minutes her burial ceremony will start. The journalists and camera people who have come to cover the funeral rites of the "Charlie Hebdo psychoanalyst" are waiting outside the cemetery.

I weave my way through the crowd of acquaintances and

strangers and try to find her family. I soon notice that in fact Elsa had several families—not just her blood relations but also a family of colleagues, of patients, a mass of friends, and on top of all that a family of readers whom her books transformed into kin. Cohabiting in this cemetery are irreconcilable and inconsolable worlds, bereaved children whose destinies have been united through the spilling of blood—the blood of magazine editors, of the customers of a kosher bakery, of a woman police officer.

There are far too many people gathered by the graves for an analytic session. I don't know where to begin, how to describe what is happening to us and all that we no longer understand. In French, to express confusion, people sometimes use a bizarre expression: "That's all Hebrew to me"—as if this particular foreign language were a little more foreign than any other, harder to master.

So why not begin there—in Hebrew.

The Hebrew word for cemetery is *a priori* absurd and paradoxical. It's *beit chaim*, the "house of life" or "the house of the living." This isn't an attempt to deny death or to conjure it away by erasing it. On the contrary: it's an attempt to send a clear message to death by placing it outside language. It's a way of making death know that for all its obvious presence in this place, it is not victorious; even here it will not have the last word.

The Jews understand this verse from the Torah, formulated in the book of Deuteronomy, as a divine injunction:

"I have put before you life and death . . . Choose life . . . " (Deuteronomy 30:19) To prove that they apply the commandment to the letter, the Jews invoke it and choose life in all circumstances.

L'Chaim, "To life!" they say each time they raise a glass, thumbing their noses at mortality. Death may all too often have knocked at their doors and tried to invite itself into their history, but Jews obstinately pretend that they can refuse it entry, saying, "Sorry, we're not in. Come back later." Even at the cemetery, they shoo death away—"Why don't you take a walk; go see if we're over there."

Let's pursue this Hebrew lesson a little further and look at a grammatical particularity. The word *chaim*, "life," is a plural. In Hebrew it doesn't exist in the singular. Hebrew indicates that each one of us has several lives, not successive but rather braided into each other like strands that cross over throughout existence and await the denouement to be unraveled. In Hebrew our lives form a tapestry until we can untie the knots by telling our stories.

"So, tell me . . . "

Elsa Cayat invited everyone she met to get to work. Each of her texts, each of the articles and books she wrote, bear the trace of what she tried to untangle for others. I wonder whether she knew that her name meant "tailor" in Hebrew and in Arabic. Across the centuries, an odd love story links Jews to textiles. Lots of Jewish jokes bear traces of this.

There's the story of a father who says to his son, "Right, now that you've done Science Po,[1] Harvard, and the Polytechnic,[2] it's time to choose: is it going to be men's fashion or women's fashion?

Perhaps in her own way, Elsa followed this ancestral tradition in treating her texts much like textiles, carefully checking for flaws thread by thread.

That day in Montparnasse Cemetery, a house of the living opened to a nation torn apart, I looked for Elsa's relatives. Her sister, Beatrice, took me by the hand and led me towards a small group of Elsa's intimates, the Cayat family and her colleagues

---

[1] Translator's note: The French Institute for Political Science is one of France's *grandes écoles,* elite and competitive specialized universities.
[2] TN: Another *grande école.*

from *Charlie Hebdo*. It was to them that Beatrice uttered words which made me wince a little.

"Let me introduce you to Delphine, our rabbi. But please don't worry, she's a *secular* rabbi."

I didn't know quite what to say, so I stayed silent. Had she said it in jest? Or was there some misunderstanding about what was expected of me? What was my function here?

I sensed what it was that Elsa's sister wanted to convey, and I understood her attempt to reassure the group.

That day, the atheism of the Cayat family, Elsa's attachment to secularism,[3] and the satirical spirit of *Charlie Hebdo*, home to her celebrated couch, should be able to be in dialogue with the words of the Jewish tradition, which I, as a rabbi, had the responsibility of bearing. There had to be a way of reconciling these two worlds, of weaving all the threads of Elsa's life together, revealing not only her own complexities but also those of a whole nation ripped asunder.

It was my task somehow to create a conversation amongst the multiple lives of this erudite, antireligious woman—Sephardi Jew, French psychoanalyst, militant feminist, loving mother, generous friend, cultivated spirit and loud-mouth—so that through her all those who in France in January 2015 thought they no longer had anything to say to each other could speak.

These many, disparate voices had to be reconciled in the attempt to reconcile all of us. Because at that moment that too was the question: how could we manage to hold together the tatters of a nation?

On that day, reciting an ancestral liturgy made up of psalms and prayers to the survivors of the *Charlie Hebdo* massacre, I

---

[3] TN: The term "laïcité" or secularism is understood by the French as a separation between the private sphere, where belief belongs, and the public sphere, where citizens are equal and ethnic or religious identity plays no role in politics or governance.

didn't become "a secular rabbi": rather, I understood that I had always been one. Some will judge the notion of a secular rabbi absurd or nonsensical, but for me the phrase expressed a profound truth that I had been struggling to formulate.

French secularism does not oppose faith with atheism. It doesn't separate those who believe that God is watching from those who believe just as firmly that he is dead or invented. It has nothing to do with that. It is founded neither on the conviction that the sky is empty nor on the conviction that it is inhabited. Rather, this secularism stems from the defense of an open world, the awareness that there is always a place for a belief that is not our own. Secularism means that our lives are not saturated with convictions or certitudes. It prevents a single faith or affiliation from taking up all the breathing space. And so, in its own way, secularism is transcendent. It affirms that a territory bigger than my belief exists, spacious enough to welcome in someone from another faith.

I've always felt Judaism carries within itself something that resonates with this idea. Jewish identity rests on "vacancy." First of all, it doesn't proselytize or try to convince others that it holds the single unique truth. Also, it has difficulty in formulating what exactly constitutes it. No one really knows what makes a Jew, let alone a "good Jew." Is it a question of origins, of practice, of belief, of a culinary tradition? Jewish identity is more than what one can say about it, and it never allows itself to be reduced to a single, restrictive definition.

To put it another way: Judaism is always bigger than "my" version of it. It preserves a free space for a conception other than my own. Thus, it has infinite transcendence in the definition which another, and then another, will give to it. Judaism guarantees within it both Elsa's place and mine, that of a non-believing Jew and that of a rabbi. Neither of us more legitimate, neither a "better" Jew nor more of a Jew than the other.

And so, if, in my Judaism, I don't make space for Elsa's, I betray it altogether. To reduce Judaism to my definition or to hers would be the same as profaning it.

Secularism is no stranger to this kind of awareness.

This is what it means to me to be a "secular rabbi": to welcome—as a blessing—the fact that my belief will never become hegemonic, neither within the French nation nor within the Jewish tradition. And to rejoice that there is enough space beneath the sky for everyone to breathe freely.

With the power of two words, Elsa's sister had expressed better than I ever could have what allowed me to stand with the people that day, to pray with the survivors of an "anti-religious" publication, and to affirm that together we could still choose life. I will always be grateful to her.

Thanks to her, I knew what story to tell, what words I could stitch together to convey, in the language of my tradition, the lives that Elsa had led. I recognized that I would have to invoke my predecessors, those whose history resonated on this January 15, 2015, in a Parisian cemetery. I understood that we had to enter an ancestral conversation, one begun much earlier in the pages of the Talmud and now waiting patiently to be shared.

This conversation started eighteen centuries ago in a small town named Yavne near Jerusalem. Several wise men took part: a certain Eliezer, one called Joshua, plus the students of their study center. Since then, generations of readers have joined in and continue to pursue the argument.

In the beginning the debate centered on an object: an oven made of stones held together with sand. The structure of this stove had the sages debating its ritual status. Was this oven vulnerable (or not) to impurities? Could it be used in all circumstances? The question may seem trivial, but the deliberations of the sages in the Talmud often have practical questions at their root, alongside legal and symbolic implications.

Rabbi Eliezer and his colleagues were not at all in agreement about the oven. Rabbi Eliezer declared the oven pure, contradicting his colleagues, and he added, "If I'm right, this tree will confirm it."

Immediately the tree was uprooted and replanted a few hundred meters from there. The rabbis of the study center, far from being impressed by this miraculous manifestation, said, "And so? What can a tree prove?"

Undiscouraged, Rabbi Eliezer went on: "If I'm right, let this river prove it."

Immediately the river that ran nearby changed its course and began to flow upstream. But Rabbi Eliezer's colleagues still refused to credit this miracle with any value and reaffirmed that their view, and not his, was the right one.

Eliezer went on with his prodigious demonstration: "If I'm right," he declared, "let the walls of the study center bend in my favor."

The walls trembled and slowly sagged towards the wise men, threatening to squash them. And now they admonished the walls, saying, "What does this have to do with you? When wise men debate, it's none of your business."

The walls interrupted their slump and stood still. They remain in that position until today, out of respect for Rabbi Eliezer and his colleagues.

As a final argument, the old sage stated in a clear voice, "If I'm right and my view is the correct one, a celestial voice will now confirm it."

Immediately, a providential voice resounded. With no equivocation it supported Eliezer, stating, "The view of Rabbi Eliezer complies with the Law."

It was then that Rabbi Joshua, who hadn't yet spoken, stood up and addressed these words to the eternal one. "The Torah is not in the heavens."

He challenged God in person, saying, "Remember, you gave

us the Law on Mount Sinai. From then on, it has been in our hands, not yours. We are in charge of its interpretation: no miracle or supernatural manifestation would be strong enough to invalidate the majority view of the sages."

The Talmud concludes this episode by telling that God started to laugh, saying, "My sons have defeated me, my sons have defeated me." (Adapted from the Babylonian Talmud, Baba Metzia 59b.)

A thunderbolt here shatters traditional religious thinking. In a simple legend, the rabbis of the Talmud upend the supposed hierarchy of power and call into question submission to a transcendent authority. According to them, the Eternal One entrusted them with the Law: it is now up to them to interpret it, even when this interpretation may go against the view of God Himself. He has deprived Himself of the power He conferred on them. This renders His intervention in history irrelevant. "Too late," they say to Him. No change to the order of the world, no miraculous phenomenon, will remove the power you have granted us.

This is how, in the second century, with a simple kitchen appliance, the rabbis set a theological revolution simmering. Divine law imposes an injunction on God to keep Himself distant. The sages even imagine that the divine rejoices in having been put in His place in this way, like a father who has taught the rules of chess to his son and loses a game to him: "Checkmate," He guffaws, amused at having been beaten. At Yavne, the Talmudic rabbis dreamt of a God with a sense of humor, prepared to withdraw from history with a laugh and eclipse himself to benefit the debating sages.

They invented a religious way of thinking which is a form of literal a-theism, a world where God doesn't intervene and where human decisions prevail when there is controversy.

"Our Father who art in heaven, / Stay there / And we will stay on earth, which is sometimes so pretty," the poet Jacques Prevert wrote in the twentieth century. Far earlier, the sages had already decreed much the same thing.

It would be altogether dishonest to transform these rabbis into atheists in the sense of "non-believers." They consecrated their lives to a God who had conferred a sacred mission on them: that of interpreting His Law and being partners in His work of creation.

The context of their debate is hardly trivial. Their revolutionary conversation takes place several decades after the destruction of the Temple in Jerusalem, at the very moment when they need to renew the idea they have had until now of the divine presence in the world. They live only a few decades after a man who, people say, crossed their region claiming that he could enact miracles, cure the sick, bring the dead back to life. In this context, there is perhaps nothing surprising in the rabbis attempting to consolidate their power by affirming that no, a miracle proves nothing if it is not part of the deliberation of men.

But whatever the historical context of this legend, it invites readers in all eras to revisit their vision of the divine. It permits them to envisage a God who laughs at his own powerlessness and takes pleasure in the audacity of the sages, even when they order him to keep his distance.

It's hard to believe that this God would be offended by the front pages of *Charlie Hébdo*, however brazen they might be, or by the columns of an insolent psychoanalyst who might tell him to get lost. Nor can I help smiling at the idea that this impertinent publication was the unwitting inheritor of a Talmudic impudence it would never have claimed as its own. Did the editors know that the God of the Talmud says too, in his own way, that it is hard to be loved by idiots?

I think of Elsa's laugh, which all of her friends have talked to me about, and of the stupidity of those who silenced it.

Were the killers aware of the obscene paradox of their act? Their belief in a God who demands vengeance and is vexed by contempt is spectacularly blasphemous. What great God could become so miserably small as to need humans to preserve His honor? To think that God is offended by mockery: isn't that the greatest possible profanity? Great is the God of humor. Small is the one who lacks it.

And that's what I said to those assembled on that January day, in a French cemetery where people who had a common belief in the grandeur of laughter, both that of God and that of humanity, had gathered. That's how we managed to cry together that morning in Montparnasse, sobbing out our sadness and clutching at humor from the depths of our despair.

On Elsa's tombstone, the words "Liberty, Equality, Fraternity" were engraved, and she rests beneath this republican triptych. For many months the extract from the Talmud that I quoted lay on her tomb: someone had put it in a plastic pouch weighed down with a stone. Eventually, it blew away.

Each time I go to Montparnasse Cemetery, I visit Elsa's grave. It is easy to get to, just beside a metallic arch, close to the central path. As tradition dictates, I place a stone on the tomb. With time, these pebbles accumulate and mark the years that pass.

Jews don't tend to leave flowers on tombs. Instead, they place these little emblematic stones; many, though, don't know the significance and origin of this custom.

A long time ago, when the dead were buried at the side of the roads or in fields, it was important to signal the presence of a tomb to travelers, and most particularly to those known by the name of Cohen. The members of this priestly family were forbidden, by biblical rule, to approach a cadaver. Contact with the dead would render them impure and thus unable to fulfil their duties as priests at the Temple, so the stones posed on burial places signaled to any passing Cohens that they had to give the site a wide berth.

With the development of closed cemeteries, the tradition of leaving small stones persisted, but more symbolic senses were attached to it. As opposed to flowers that wilt, stones remain and signify the strength of memory. They tell of the inalterable place that the dead have in the lives of those who have survived them.

Then too, the word pebble in Hebrew has a hidden aspect and a powerful symbolic weight. A small stone is known as an *ebben*, and this word, split into its parts, reveals a combination of *ab* and *ben*, meaning parent and child.

To place a stone on a tomb is to declare to the one who lies there that he or she is being written into a line of heritage, placed in a chain of generations that prolongs their history. The stone talks of filiation, real or fictional, but always true.

Do the children of January 2015 bear a permanent scar? What legacy did we take on that day? It's still too soon to say. The events turned us into bereaved children who will need years to understand all that we owe to those who died in that savage moment. I often think of Elsa's daughter, one of those children, and of her grief.

Her silhouette on that January 15 remains very clear to me. She is a very young woman, elegant: dark hair, high heels. She is wrapped in a fur coat the same color as her hair and which gives her something of a Hollywood air. I imagine her choosing her clothes and each of her accessories with great care that morning, like a little girl donning the costume of a *grande dame* to disguise her sorrow.

Elsa's daughter was on my right as her mother's coffin was

lowered into the ground. Side by side, we recited the Kaddish, the prayer for the bereaved, and threw a handful of earth onto the coffin. It was then that she turned to me, and with a great sob, asked, "So that's it: Mum's not coming back again?"

At the heart of this national tragedy and collective mourning, as millions joined spontaneous demonstrations and heads of state from around the world walked through Paris, we had perhaps forgotten one essential: explaining to a daughter that her mother was gone forever. In collective or national mourning, something is inevitably taken away from the family or loved ones of the victims, something they have a right to: the acknowledgement of a pain we can't begin to imagine, and of words which carry truth.

I told Elsa's daughter that no, her mother wouldn't come back. But I added that she was all around us. She was in the sophisticated coat worn by a child who seemed to promise, "I will be what I have decided to be." She was in the unconscious of her patients, who, thanks to her, were able to tell different stories. She was in the antic laughter of inconsolable friends who refuse to renounce humor and to allow death to triumph.

Coming out of the cemetery on that January day, I met the illustrator Jul, who was part of the *Charlie Hebdo* editorial team. He took my arm and, with a wink, whispered into my ear, "Just in case these attacks continue, I'd like to book you for my funeral. It would make my mother so happy . . . "

And in this house of the living, I thought I could hear the echoes of Elsa's booming laugh amidst our sobs.

MARC

Ghost Clothes

Elsa won't come back," I had said to her daughter.
I was wrong.

In June 2017, two years after the *Charlie Hebdo* assassinations, I get a call from a family who have just lost one of their members. Marc was fifty-nine: he left behind his parents, a partner, and a son. Through them I discovered the brilliant man, far too young to die, whom I was to accompany to his grave at their sides.

Meeting family and preparing a funeral ceremony is a sacred time, even though that can sound trivial in the writing. But those few hours or days spent with the newly bereaved are truly a "sacred" time, as the word in Hebrew implies. *Kadosh*, "sacred," literally means "separate" or "apart," and the disappearance of a loved one thrusts those left behind into a "separate" time. Linearity is interrupted.

Jewish tradition has it that between the time of death and the moment of burial, a candle is placed near the body of the deceased. This candle signifies the presence of the soul, which is still alive. The rite contains a deep truth: something in the life of the dead person is incandescent during these few days. It's a time during which the life that has gone sparkles with particular brightness. All those who come near notice it. This light could set the world on fire or allow us to see what has been totally obscured.

This is why the conversations I have with family in this out-of-time time are decisive. As a rabbi, I know I have very little time to discern this light through the spoken words and gestures, the narratives and the silences of those who make up the dead person's close circle. I have to capture what this light reveals, whom it illuminates, what shadows it holds, and the way in which it vibrates.

I know that some will see this as a form of religious nonsense or magical thinking. I'm not talking here, though, of a belief in the eternity of the soul or in life after death, but of a concrete and rational awareness that these rites can bring a sense of destiny to the life of the dead, as long as we speak of them without betrayal.

The writer André Malraux famously wrote that "the tragedy of death is that it transforms life into destiny." Death definitely has this power, thanks to the words and rites that accompany it. It creates a narrative that constructs life as a kind of monument, built on foundations laid with the last breath. Nonetheless, as opposed to what Malraux suggests, it seems to me that, in these sacred moments, it isn't necessary to invoke tragedy. It is possible to think differently about the memorial that begins to be erected before our eyes.

There are many other ways of transforming life into destiny. Death is often a tragedy, especially when it erupts at a moment that seems inconceivable, far too soon, or when its violence obliterates everything in its path. Too often a brutal end can kidnap the entirety of an existence, reducing it to its final outcome. But there is a way of preventing death from stealing the full story of a life:

Never tell the story of a life by its end but by everything within it that considered itself without end.

Remember to talk about everything that might have been before saying what will no longer be.

I remember a scene from the 2010 romantic comedy *The*

Names of Love by the director Michel Leclerc. In a flashback to his adolescence, the main character, son of wartime deportees, takes part in a school ceremony to erect a plaque to the children who died in concentration camps. As the teacher explains the significance of this commemoration, the teenage boy shocks his classmates by interjecting, "If I had been killed and had to walk past this thing every day, reminding me how horrible it was to have been killed, I'm not sure I'd like it. It would be better, for instance, to remember the day the children first ate whipped cream. You could write on the plaque, 'In this school, children ate whipped cream for the first time.' I think that would be nicer for them."

The boy's remarks anger his teacher, who doesn't understand that this provocation contains a truth worth contemplating: there are many ways of telling the stories of our departed, even when their death is dramatic. Perhaps we have to make sure that our memory stays faithful to the complexity of their life, which can never be summed up by the tragedy of their end.

I have often wished for myself and those I love that on the day of our burial our lives can be told in a genre other than tragedy, that we can be evoked in other registers, that our stories can be seen as thrillers or romances, as myths, or even as comedies; as long as we are not boiled down to mere death, everyone will be able to feel how very alive we once were.

Sometimes at a funeral the speeches miss the life itself, or the celebrant misjudges the tone. That's happened to me. I remember having the feeling that I had completely failed in my eulogy of a man who deserved better. I hadn't known how to grasp the salient elements of his life. His brothers and sisters had come to prepare the ceremony several days earlier and had struggled to answer my questions, as if entire facets of his personality eluded them, as if he had been a stranger until the end.

"Did he have any passions?"

"Not really, not to our knowledge."

"Who were the people who really counted for him?"

"Hard to say."

"What were his dreams?"

"As far as we know, he really didn't have any."

The answers to all these questions came only during the ceremony itself: in other words, too late. The man we were commemorating had been loved passionately; his family just didn't know it. His friends and lovers, now gathered together, were a testament to this. They were his real family, they were the ones to whom he had confided his dreams, but they hadn't come to talk to me.

With the strict compartmentalization of his life, this man's blood relatives had somehow passed him by. So, on the day of his funeral, I was the spokesperson for ignorance, the conduit of missed opportunity, the witness to an encounter that had never taken place. I had to take this failure into account, gracefully or not, at the cemetery: not to negate the boundary he had constructed to separate the people in his life, but also to lend an ear to what had transpired on the other side of the invisible wall, to listen to what I hadn't known.

Marc's funeral wasn't like that. Marc knew how to bring together all those who counted in his life. People on that day talked of his great humanity. I noticed just how much love there was in his life: his love of medicine and care for others, his love of writing and of his family, the love of his friends and of all those with whom he had powerful attachments and affinities. One of these friends had recently surfaced again and asked to speak.

On the eve of Marc's burial, as I was writing his funeral oration, I received a message from his family. They wanted to add a detail to our conversation, an anecdote they had forgotten to share with me. I ought to know, they said, that for several months Marc had exchanged emails with a certain Elsa Cayat, the psychoanalyst killed during the attack on *Charlie Hebdo*. This correspondence had been important to him, and the family wanted to publish the messages in book form. They attached a copy of this electronic conversation, interrupted in 2015.

I had thought Elsa would not come back. I was wrong. One evening she returned true to form, knocking at my door, or rather at the screen of my computer, to haunt my spirit and help me write. I opened the attachment Marc's family had sent.

It was very late, and I trembled at the thought of what I was going to read. I even asked myself whether I had the right to do so. It seemed Marc and Elsa had exchanged many emails throughout 2014, the last full year of Elsa's life.

I don't think I'm betraying them to share a little of what these letters contained: they were destined for publication. Marc told her his memories and reflected on them. Elsa in response drew on her psychoanalytic experience. Together they had arrived at a theme to explore and write about, a theme which would one day be the subject of their book. Throughout 2014, these two had conversed about death. Needless to say, neither of them suspected it would visit each of them in turn so soon.

And that's how, one night in the summer of 2017, a haunted manuscript made its way to me by email: an epistolary dialogue between two beings who couldn't have suspected that its post-mortem and first reading would be carried out by the rabbi who would bury them both.

In evoking death, it's as if they were telling me what they wanted to hear in their funeral orations. Perhaps they were inviting me to meet them. Never before had a revenant revealed itself to me through letters, let alone emails.

Revenants. This is an apt term for ghosts because that's

exactly what they do: *revenir*, return. Coming back to us until we give in and see them and finally talk about them.

So, let's be led by them and go back ourselves.

All children play at ghosts. I remember hiding hundreds of times behind the living-room curtains at my grandparents' and crying "Oooooo!" In our childhood films and cartoons, these ghosts are alike: silhouettes enveloped in swirling white fabric. But the origins and symbolism of these ghosts are often lost in popular culture. Their white robes are in fact a throwback to an ancestral Jewish rite: the enveloping of the dead in white shrouds.

In Jewish custom, the deceased are not buried in their city suits or their Sunday best. Instead, they are prepared, washed, and then dressed in a white tunic for burial. This garment represents the garb worn by the High Priest officiating in the Temple of Jerusalem some two thousand years ago.

The Torah describes very precisely how the High Priest purified himself, carried out his ablutions, and put on his robe to ready himself for the altar where he would confront the Creator. At the Temple, the Cohen was the man who could come closest to the divine, the only one who could enter the inner sanctuary of the Holy of Holies, in other words, who had the right to face the invisible deity. In Jewish tradition, every man on the day of his burial is a high priest: he is washed and clothed, his body enveloped in a shroud representing the priestly vestments, as he too prepares to meet God face to face.

So, our childhood ghosts are made in the image of this funereal clergy who haunt our collective memories. They replay the rites—but with one difference. In the Jewish tradition, a final detail finishes off the preparation of the dead: the shroud must be sewn up at its extremities just before the body is to be buried. The garment of the dead is closed shut, and these last stitches seal the deceased's departure.

This final moment in the funeral preparations can have unexpected repercussions on the everyday life of Jewish families, including my own. When I was a child, if I lost a button or my clothing was torn, and the repair had to be done quickly, my mother would give me a surprising and rather comic command: I was to chew energetically and exaggerate my facial movements as she sewed. It took me years to understand the superstition behind this seemingly anodyne order, which in reality was dramatic: it harked back to the prohibition of sewing fabric on a living person, since this is an action carried out on the dead.

It was thus necessary to ward off bad luck, or more precisely to send a very clear message to the angel of death, just in case he happened to be in the vicinity. Imagine if he witnessed this act of sewing: he might conclude that he was in the presence of a dead person. The exaggerated chewing would signal that no, the person was very much alive. "Sorry, there's been a misunderstanding—it was just a quick repair." That's the way you invite death to come back later. Much, much later.

This is what the ghost in so many films and in popular culture represents: the white flowing form is a dead person wrapped in a shroud, cloaked in funeral vestments that have been badly sewn, or not sewn up at all.

Because no one has finished the seams, the phantom can't leave this world. It's held here and carries on haunting, awaiting the final stitches that will allow it to depart for good. *Rouach refaim*, which literally means "released spirit," is the term for ghosts in Hebrew. These spirits' stitching has come apart, and because they still bear the traces of their frayed histories, they must return. They need to unpick things, to see their history mended by those who survive them.

In M. Night Shyamalan's film *The Sixth Sense*, a child repeats to the adults around him the terrifying phrase, "I see dead people." If viewers shudder, it's because they're forced to ask themselves whether they've simply refused to see the ghosts around them. What if we were all able to see these revenants, if seeing them simply meant paying more attention, watching the curtains move?

Again, this isn't a question of literal belief in a life after death or in the presence of souls wandering about old houses. It means recognizing, rationally, that we all live with ghosts.

These could be restless apparitions from our personal, family, or collective histories, or the ghostly remnants of countries in which we were born, of cultures which have given us shelter, of stories told to or kept from us, sometimes even of the languages we speak.

I come across these specters almost every time I welcome a mourner to my office. The shadows inhabit the stories people share with me, the family secrets they confide, or the curses that travel from one generation to the next. Ghosts like anniversaries: they show up at regular intervals in families where narratives are repeated, especially to those who are convinced they know nothing of their family history—or worse, think it has nothing to do with them.

Such ghosts have always existed in families, but sometimes historical events multiply their number. War tends to create a great many of them. In Jewish families in particular, ghosts live for a long time and in excellent health, well-nourished on stories rich in trauma, ideal for their development.

There are the stubborn phantoms of the Shoah, the unmarked dead; those of forced conversions and hidden children, like the Marranos of the Spanish Inquisition and their descendants of silence, of all that it was necessary to keep quiet about in order to be saved. There's everything the grandparents didn't talk about and everything no one dared ask them about, the phantoms of fear and exile alongside those of guilt. It's not hard to convene a crowd of the revenants who inhabit our lives.

At every stage—birth, bar mitzvah, marriage, mourning—there they are on the guest list, amongst the first to arrive. They resurge whenever matters of lineage come into play, and if something in the family is being tied up or ruptured, sealed or ripped apart, here they come. Any event that binds or unravels the family summons them. As it must. Ghosts are ever in search of the missing threads that would suture our histories to theirs.

In the old Jewish legends, these ghosts were called dybbuks. The word comes from a Hebrew root *dabaq*, which means to stick or to cling. These presences arise from our past and suddenly adhere to our lives like thermal adhesive tape applied to threadbare fabric. The two textiles merge and become one.

The dybbuk grafts itself to our lives. It is neither good nor evil, neither well nor ill-intentioned. It latches onto our stories like a parasite. It might hinder or help, might prevent or abet us taking a different path. In certain Jewish stories, the ghost might trip up its host or get them out of a tight spot. This dybbuk inhabits the pages of Isaac Bashevis Singer's books, and so many others. In Romain Gary's 1967 novel *The Dance of Genghis Cohn*, the dybbuk, the ghost of a Jew assassinated at Auschwitz, ruins the life of a former Nazi. The dybbuk is also prominent in traditional Jewish literature.

The Rabbi Joseph Karo (1448–1475), the celebrated author of the *Shulchan Aruch*, or Code of Jewish Law, was convinced that his wife's infertility had been cured by a dybbuk. According to him, this spirit "glued" to the soul of his wife had personally furnished the seed she needed to become fertile.

So, it would seem that ghosts aren't always malevolent. Sometimes, they tell you a story, your own story, and explain that it's merely a reprise of their own.

In the very first email that Marc sends to Elsa, someone slips in who will come to take up a lot of room: the ghost of the little boy he once was. In fact, their discussion takes wing from a childhood event he narrates. From the earliest lines of their exchange, Marc tells Elsa of his first encounter with the idea of death:

I must be around ten. I'm in my bed. This scene comes very precisely into my memory like a film. It's late, and I can't fall asleep.

My parents are watching Channel Two, which has recently switched to color, while I, alone in my room in the dark, twist and turn under my sheets. I don't realize it yet, but my unconscious has opened a door which will never again close. Goodbye to the carefree days of childhood, all those beautiful years in which time didn't count, where time flowed away in long minutes, or long hours of waiting. That night I realized that I had lived ten years of my life. Ten years already consumed, like a candle which inexorably melts towards extinction. Like a sand timer you can't turn around. Once more like that, and I would be twenty. As much again, and I would be forty . . . and once more, a quantity which it seems ridiculous to count, eighty years old . . . in other words at the end. At my death.

A small boy of ten has an anxiety attack as he becomes conscious of the inevitability of death. This child who has suddenly discovered mortality calls for his mother in the middle of the night, and she comes to reassure him. This child, become man and now dead well before reaching "the end" as it was calculated, recounts to this woman, who a few months later will die, just what had terrified him at the age of ten: at the start of his story, he already knew how it would end.

Elsa replies to him and suggests that that night offers a key to understanding a story that goes much further back. According to her, this night carries the trace of a ghost. "What is the feeling of panic?" she asks. "It's a very powerful sense of abandonment which reignites something you weren't told about *your* history. This fear of death is a desire for death; the fear of being abandoned is translated into a wish to abandon oneself definitively."

As I read these few lines of their exchange and pass them on to you, I am not sure whether I'm doing them justice or betraying them. I can't altogether tell if making their voices resonate is an act of homage or of disrespect.

Nothing is more dangerous than making the dead speak. Yet nothing is more sacrilegious than to silence them. But I won't go any further with this.

I won't speak on behalf of Elsa and Marc. I hope I have known how to be faithful to their worlds in describing them without distorting their conversation. I would just like to express my gratitude to them. For in truth, and entirely unexpectedly, their correspondence from the other side of death and never intended for me has allowed me to revisit elements of my own history. Perhaps it is because of the way their lives echoed within mine that I found the ability to accompany them.

In a curious fashion, it seemed to me when reading their emails that they weren't only asking me to confront their hauntings but equally to face my own fears. Maybe the ghosts in their exchange were no more theirs than mine, and they were inviting me to hear them.

As I read their correspondence, I knew that I too would have to gather together my ghosts in the way that Marc had convened his. After all, the realization of death which had showed itself one night to a child and stopped him from sleeping hadn't just found Mark. It had paid me a visit too. It was a long time ago when I was nearly ten, during the night of a childhood still hidden behind my grandparents' curtains.

I was spending my holidays in Nancy in my paternal grandparents' apartment. My brother and I, permanent rivals, as children close in age often are, were ramping up our tactics as we vied for the status of favorite grandchild or model heir. Jealousy often cut our games short, and our arguments were legendary.

That day, my brother had received a gift that fascinated me. It was a chemistry set which allowed you to dip a toy in resin to give it a shiny plastic coating. The object then took on the aspect of a paperweight or a collector's item.

I don't precisely recall the appearance of this solidified material, nor even its actual appeal . . . but I do distinctly remember its heady odor and my stubborn jealousy. This strange olfactory memory overpowers other recollections.

The end of the afternoon arrived, and the odor of resin emanating from one of the objects my brother had placed on the dining room table attracted me irresistibly. For a reason that now evades me, I brought this object first to my nose then to my mouth. The plastic was a little soft in consistency, and I suddenly wanted to taste it. Finally, having chewed on an extremity, I swallowed a small piece.

I can't quite remember exactly what followed. I only know that when night fell and bedtime arrived, I was suddenly seized by a terror mingled with certainty. This little bit of swallowed resin had obviously poisoned me. I had the absolute and desperate conviction that nothing could save me. That night would be my last. I would die. It was certain. I was condemned.

For hours, I cried in bed, refusing to tell my grandparents anything about my "revelation." It was out of the question to announce my imminent death: the idea of causing them pain was intolerable. I had to confront this last night of my life alone and hide the reasons for my fast-approaching demise.

For the first time in my life, I had the wild idea of turning to someone who might provide the only possible salvation. For the first time in my life, so short yet so soon to be over, I decided to pray. I began an awkward conversation with a God never spoken of in my house. And since nothing was ever said about him, I knew nothing of the art of speaking to him.

The lack of prayer in my house may sound surprising. After all, my grandfather was a rabbi, or at least had been to a rabbinical school before becoming a teacher. He had a patriarchal manner, and he was considered by many to be a pious man. His silence about God was a trademark of his brand of "Israelite" Judaism, which centered on a republican rationalism doubled up with a strong attachment to all the domestic rites of Judaism; these, though, were practiced with extreme discretion, with nothing about individual beliefs or practices conveyed to either the outside world or to the members of one's own family.

It was under his roof that night, and without saying anything to him, that I formulated the very first prayer of my life. From my child's point of view, a negotiation with an unknown God was my only hope of escaping death. A little girl had come knocking on His door with the old refrain, "If you save me, I promise to . . . "

It's impossible now for me to remember the precise content of the solemn pledges I made on that night. I simply remember having the sensation that I was making a pact with something larger than me. I prayed, I cried, and I prayed some more.

And that night, God answered me. He didn't manifest as a flaming bush that burns without consuming itself. He didn't thrust Mount Sinai up into my room nor proclaim the ten commandments. Instead, he sent me a savior.

Late that night, my grandfather crossed the apartment. I heard him walking the length of the hall and then he appeared in my room, as if he knew what I was going through.

He sat at the foot of my bed and with great tenderness invited me to share my fear, in other words, my fear of death. I remember telling him about the theft of my brother's toy, the temptation, and then the supreme transgression of having tasted the irresistible plasticated resin; about my guilt, then my terror, and the death which had got mixed up in it all. Confession doesn't really exist in Judaism, except for the one that immediately precedes death. Despite knowing nothing of this tradition, I was submitting to it.

Years later, and in my turn a rabbi, I can't help but wonder what my grandfather must have heard that night in his grandchild's narrative.

Could he see anything other in it than an evident echo of an ancient Bible story? Nearly all the motifs were invoked there, as if resurrected in the terror of a child playing out an ancient tale known by all, but not yet by her.

And this story tells that in the beginning humans were placed in a garden, that Eden of original innocence, where a world created in seven days is still promised eternal serenity. Those childish humans in the paradise of Eden don't heed God's words of warning: "Of every tree of the garden, thou mayest freely eat / But of the tree of the knowledge of good and evil, thou shalt not eat of it: for in the day that thou eatest thereof thou shalt surely die." (Genesis 2:16–17.)

Is there any way in which this interdiction could not have been transgressed? The humans end up succumbing and tasting. And so, the Torah says, their eyes "were opened," and they understood that the warning had been more subtle than it seemed. No human dies immediately from eating the forbidden fruit—neither Adam nor Eve nor their descendants. But in that moment, knowledge was acquired: the awareness that death will come one day. Recognizing their mortality, humans hide, in a garden, or sometimes under their covers. They're terrified. And God, who knows very well where to find them, asks, "Where art thou?" (Genesis, 3:9.)

This is not a question of geography: it's existential. As humanity opens its eyes to death, it knows full well where it is:

it has been torn from the world of its birth, from its innocence, and is forever expelled from the garden of its origins.

When my grandfather heard my fear, he got up and did something which changed the course of history, which is to say that of my personal genesis. He went to look at the dining-room table to find what was left of the chewed object I had left there as discretely as possible. He then came back to sit at my side. Looking me straight in the eyes, he put the object in his mouth and bit off a large chunk, which he chewed and swallowed. Then he kissed me tenderly, wished me good night and left.

I understood that night not that the plastic I had swallowed was harmless, since nothing then could persuade me of that. I had a far more essential revelation: I learned that my grandfather, the greatest sage in my world, would accompany me in my exile. He was telling me that, at my side, he would leave Eden again, and that, in the face of death, he wouldn't abandon me.

Much later that night I finally fell asleep.

Waking up the next morning, I had the sense that I had been saved. My grandfather never spoke to me again of that episode. Nor did I ever raise it. Confronted with this secret, we became Israelites again, people who kept their beliefs, their practices, and even their fears to themselves. But I think something between us changed forever. We had sealed a pact.

When I think of this childhood memory, the adult I have become laughs and shrugs. She would like to say to the terrified little girl, "You weren't in danger. It was your fertile imagination and sense of guilt making you scared."

I also know that the child who speaks within me from time to time lived something particularly real that night: an encounter with death.

That child knows, as Marc did and reflected on in his letter to Elsa, that in the darkness a door opened on the terrifying knowledge that death would come back one day.

That open door undoubtedly has a lot to do with what I became. Through it came questions and quests, fears, and prayers, but also trust in the idea that in this world there is the possibility of salvation. That hope carries many names. Some call it God, but Jews decided not to name Him. His name is ineffable, and the refusal to utter it is a recognition that His power is immense and beyond the limits of words. He takes on many faces and characteristics, sometimes that of a savior, at other times that of a secret.

I did know from then on that I had risked nothing that night, that I wasn't going to die of poisoning, but I also know that in that half-light I was saved, by a small prayer and a great man.

From the moment I was expelled from the Eden of childhood, I knew that there was no way back. At the cusp of ten, in a panic attack, I became a "survivor."

I hear Elsa's voice. She responds to me with the very words she addressed to Marc, and, through him, to all those who might one day wish to read her: "What is the feeling of panic?" she asks. "It's a very powerful sense of abandonment which reignites something you weren't told about *your* history." At my paternal grandparents' house one night, I encountered death. It came as a signal that I hadn't been told everything about my own history. To warn me that my garden contained many ghosts and secrets that grew there like trees. Amongst them was one that held the fruit of the knowledge of good and absolute evil, of the knowledge of a history never told. That was the tree of the survivors to whom I was born.

That tree grew elsewhere, not at my paternal grandparents',

but in the ravaged garden belonging to my maternal family. I was the fruit of trees burnt to ash at Auschwitz, where no one had ever taken me and of which nothing had been spoken. From the surviving trees that had been uprooted and planted elsewhere, a bitter sap exuded. It made its way to me.

The ten-year-old me had decided to taste that memory, ready to be poisoned by it.

Thirty years later, seeing off first Elsa and then Marc, I was compelled by the power of their exchange and personal histories to revisit my own.

SARAH AND SARAH

The Basket of Generations

Her son telephones me.
She has just died, and he wants me to conduct the funeral tomorrow in a cemetery near Paris. "We aren't religious," he says, "but she would have wanted a Kaddish." I've heard this sentence so often that I've also learned to read all the meanings it may be charged with. There are variations on the theme: one is, "You know, we'd like a traditional funeral, even if we aren't 'good Jews' really."

I've stopped explaining that nothing makes you more of a Jew than saying that you aren't a good one, and that it's very Jewish to believe you aren't the person you ought to be. In fact, generally it would be more suspect if you *did* think you were exactly as you "should" be. Judaism doesn't require its adherents to pass a final exam. It doesn't have a roll of honor or hand out certificates, and every Jew knows that to another Jew his kitchen wouldn't be kosher enough or his practice strict enough. So be it.

He starts our conversation with an apology, and when he says, "I'm not a good Jew," I feel like saying, "Me neither. Now stop showing off." But this isn't the moment for jokes. That said . . .

Two rabbis are in the back of a cab in New York City. One says to the other: "I'm small and mediocre. I'm non-existent." The other raises the stakes. "I'm dust of dust, mere vaporous smoke, without shape, utterly ridiculous." The cab driver turns towards them and exclaims. "Come on now, if you two rabbis, with your wisdom, are dust and smoke, then I'm a nothing of nothings, an abominable bit of garbage, mere residue." The two sages look at each other and shrug: "Who does this guy think he is?"

In a thousand ways, and even in its humor, Jewish wisdom affirms that greatness is not to be spoken aloud, least of all by whomever has it. You have to be truly great to be able to call yourself small. The conviction that you are as you "should" be paradoxically makes you a little less legitimate.

My meeting with the less than good Jew takes place in a café I often go to. This may seem incongruous, but I need a little life around me to talk about the dead. People raise their glasses, and I'm tempted to say *L'Chaim*.

The man arrives on his own. When he begins to speak, his dead mother Sarah joins us, carried in the words of her only son. She listens to him discretely as he recounts her life. When she was alive, she didn't tell him much about it. I recognize her straight away: the silence of elderly Jews is very familiar to me. It always spoke loudly in my childhood. It's the silence of survivors.

I know from the start of our conversation that her life can't really be told, but her son tries, nevertheless. He wants to tell me who she was. Yet, as we both know, neither the words nor the dates can begin to describe what happened to her. We could talk about it just as well if we stopped talking. Her life spans a century and possibly a little further. According to the official French documents, made out in the Fifties, his mother was ninety-seven years old. According to his own calculations, she was probably a lot older. The dates don't align.

In fact, nothing quite hangs together. The story he brings to me is a patchwork of events, each more tragic than the last. The misfortunes that rained down on Sarah are infinitely greater than a hundred years can contain.

There is her birth in Hungary, near Budapest, as the only child of Jewish tradespeople. Her parents die, murdered, while she is still small, and she is given over to an aunt. She grows up in poverty, gets married, and becomes a mother herself to a daughter called Rivka. Very soon her husband grows ill and dies. War tightens the vice. In the summer of 1944, Sarah, her aunt, and little Rivka are deported to Auschwitz. On their arrival at the camp, they are immediately separated. Rivka is torn from Sarah's arms, and she watches her beloved daughter herded away from her, together with her aunt, towards the gas chambers. Sarah survives the camp and by chance ends up in Paris in 1945. She takes on any number of small jobs and tries to construct some semblance of a life. She manages to get papers by fudging dates and falsifying sworn statements. She then meets Misha, he, too, a survivor. They settle together and have a son, this "bad Jew" who is telling me, as best he can, the story of his mother. Sarah and Misha don't get on and shout a lot, in Yiddish. They separate. Sarah spends the next forty years alone, working long hours for a meagre salary and a negligible pension. Her only comforts are her son's rare visits and the even rarer visits of her two grandchildren.

"My mother was very hard," he says to me, as if one could be anything other and survive the existence she had. Most descendants of Holocaust survivors are no strangers to this characteristic toughness. Did their relatives survive because they were tough, or did they grow hard in order to survive? No one can really say.

Communication in these families is often complex, more shouted than spoken. A friend from a similar background confessed to me one day, "For a long time I used to think that Yiddish was a language you couldn't speak without barking."

I listen to this son evoking his mother, and I ask myself how I'm going to be able to tell her story to her loved ones at the cemetery the next day. What will resonate? What should I say to her descendants, to this assembled group, some of whom may know very little of this twentieth-century *misérable*, a Cosette of the Hungarian ghetto? Should I tell the story of a mother or the history of a century of which we are all the children?

Should I say that we are sending off one of the last of her kind, that her generation is leaving us, that soon there will be no survivors or first-hand witnesses left?

Obviously, I have to do all of this and emphasize how the history of one woman bears the history of all people, not just in her own time, but also long after, as we live with the terrible knowledge of what took place. To speak of Sarah, one has to speak of history, and not only her own; we have to remind ourselves, through her story, of what humans have done to other humans, so that all generations will remember.

In Hebrew, the word for "generation" is *dor*. It's a word that is omnipresent in liturgy and prayers. *Midor ledor*, "from generation to generation," *bechol dor vador* "to each generation," Eternal One, we sing of You, glorify You, put our confidence in You, know that You will intervene in our favor . . . Many are the references to this intergenerational hope and confidence in the prayer books.

If you know Jewish history and its series of tragedies and catastrophes, you might ask with a touch of irony whether we'd notice any difference if each generation *stopped* thanking God for his miraculous intervention.

Although we translate *dor* as "generation," it in fact signifies something a little more complex. It literally means the action of weaving a basket. The image is simple and striking, evoking rows of reeds or straw intertwined with the preceding row. A basket is always made from the bottom to the top, each new row attached to the one that generated it, anchored in it, in order to constitute in its turn, the support the next row needs.

The metaphor is easy to understand: a generation in Hebrew is a strand of the basket. It relies on the strength of the preceding row and anticipates the consolidation of the next.

As in basket-making, so in our families: a single weakened or broken row can put the whole structure in danger and lead to collapse, from top to bottom or bottom to top.

The Shoah created great gaps in Sarah's generational basket: the family couldn't easily be woven together. War did the same to mine and to that of so many others. Intense grief led to gaps that were patched up to give the basket a semblance of form.

I've often met children of survivors who were so damaged that the family basket was upended: the children born after the catastrophe became parents to those who had given birth to them. The direction of history was inverted: the new generation had somehow to work backwards to reunite with the strands of their parents' histories.

Those whose parents had lost children during the war faced an even more intricate repair: they had not only to become the parents of their parents but also replace lost older siblings, grasping for ghosts while also anchoring the devastated beings who had given them birth.

These children born after the Shoah were entrusted with the impossible mission to parent their parents, and they took it upon themselves both to fiercely protect and to admonish them.

Often, they also sought to mend them. Shoah descendants or not, most children attempt to do this, and at one point or another see themselves as saviors, convinced they can bring redemption to their ancestors and correct everything that went wrong before. This infant-Messiah syndrome is multiplied tenfold in traumatized families.

Short of reviving the dead, tragedies and bereavements make this exercise of reparation at once senseless and doomed to failure. Some understand how unrealizable the project is and end up fleeing, attempting to weave a new life elsewhere in order to survive their survivor parents.

But it's not easy for a son who leaves his survivor parents or distances himself from them. He risks spending years berating himself for being both a bad Jew and a bad son.

One by one, the survivors die. We realize that there are so many things we didn't know, so much they didn't say, and we didn't ask about. Sometimes they vanish without revealing their original names or their place of birth, let alone the story of their murdered family. Sometimes we don't even know how old they are, as in Sarah's case. We then spend the rest of our lives wondering if the scant information we have is as riddled with untruths as the declarations made post-war to the French state.

The day after my conversation with Sarah's son, I arrived at the cemetery early. I wanted to see what this family and its scattered strands looked like. I wanted to know with whom Sarah's son had made a life far from his mother: who were the friends who had come to shore him up, what were they like? Were they Jewish? Did they share a little of his history or did they know nothing of it? To whom would I soon be telling this cursed tale?

I edge my way into a group at the entrance to the cemetery. They were waiting for the start of the ceremony and instructions from the undertakers. Sarah's son wasn't there yet, and I decided simply to wait with the first arrivals, as if I were a mere acquaintance, the better to observe them. The small group swelled minute by minute. Some knew each other and exchanged small talk; others waited in silence. No one said anything to me.

Finally, an attendant, who had evidently just had permission for the funeral to proceed, came to find us. "Those here for Madame Marchand can now advance to the burial site."

The little group started to move forward. It took a few seconds for me to realize that I had joined the wrong cortege and infiltrated someone else's burial. Unless I was going to foist Sarah's history on them to tell them a little of her, I had no business with these strangers mourning another loss entirely.

Sarah's son arrived later, when the coffin I had wanted to follow was probably already in the ground. I saw him coming into the cemetery, and, of course, I said nothing about his mother's "first burial."

He came straight towards me with a "Let's go." He signaled to the funeral director, and our convoy, the real one, slowly moved forward. Slowly enough for me to understand that at this burial there would be only him and me. Sarah's son had come alone, completely alone.

The night before he had said to me, "We are not religious, but she would have wanted a Kaddish." Did he not know that in order to recite this prayer we needed at least ten people to form what is known as a *minyan?* I said nothing and walked with him towards the plot.

In Jewish tradition, the Kaddish refers not only to the prayer spoken for the dead but equally to the person who leads its recital. A father or mother can very well introduce their son with the words, "Here is my Kaddish"; in other words, here is the person who will one day recite the prayer at the edge of my tomb.

And so, that day, I found myself alone with Sarah's only Kaddish.

On the cemetery path, a few steps away from the open grave, the coffin was placed between us. We faced each other. On one side, the man who yesterday evening had told me everything he knew about his mother; on the other, the woman who would repeat this to him.

I had thought I would be addressing others. I would be talking to men and women who, through my words, would get to know Sarah. I imagined I would deliver a beautiful tribute. Ridiculous vanity, on my part. I ended up simply talking of this woman to the very man who had told me everything I now knew about her.

What I did was to translate his words into my own language, so that he would hear them differently. I told him of his mother, of the world before his time, of the bereavements, the stolen child.

I think that I had never better understood my role as a celebrant at a cemetery: to accompany the grieving, not to teach them something they don't yet know but to translate what they have told me so that they in turn can actually *hear* it. In that way, the narrative that left their lips returns to their ears by the intermediary of a voice that isn't theirs, or at least not altogether theirs. It's a voice that creates a dialogue between their words and an ancestral tradition, transmitted from generation to generation, to both "good" and "bad" Jews, and especially to those who are doing their best.

So here we are again. The rabbi utters the words of tradition that have been transmitted from generation to generation, *midor ledor*, and we help weave the family basket together by adding new strands.

In this way the story of a man or a woman is mended a little, repaired by the renewed listening of its heirs. This is the work, the linkage, that happens at the grave's edge.

That day, I told a man who his mother had been, based only on what he had already told me. And yet—and I don't quite know how to explain this—it's as if, through the telling and listening, another story had been articulated and taken shape between us.

Sarah's son moved towards the coffin and caressed the wood that enveloped his mother. He cried for a long time. "What a life she had!" he murmured. I don't know to what extent he had only just discovered this.

We then stood there in silence for a long time. I didn't ask Sarah's son why he had come alone, where his children were, or why he hadn't thought it a good idea to bring them to their grandmother's funeral. I didn't need to ask him. I knew the answer perfectly well. Once, I too had been a child like him.

I had simply put aside, in my role as rabbi, how familiar Sarah's story was to me, how much it was also my own, or rather that of another Sarah, my grandmother.

A young Jewish woman from the Carpathians, deported to Auschwitz-Birkenau with a child she would never see again; a survivor walled in by silence. After the war, she gave birth to my mother and my aunt and said nothing—certainly not to them— of her story or of her life before the war. To survive her, they went off to look for her elsewhere, and, in turn, told nothing of this history to their children, acting as though the torn and tattered family basket could still be carried about and more or less keep its shape.

When my grandmother died, I was kept at a distance. I wasn't invited to her funeral. I was twelve or thirteen, but not for a second did anyone consider it might be right that I attend. I didn't need to know her story. It had been decided the Kaddish would be recited in the absence of the grandchildren. I don't know how many people accompanied my mother that day. There was no question of me being part of the procession, nor even that I might ask to join it.

My mother prohibited our entering a cemetery. It's an old Ashkenazi superstition: children should not be brought close to death. Underlying this, I suppose, is the notion that death will thus leave them alone.

I remember that when I was very little, an old lady who sometimes came to look after us decided one day to take my brother and me to leave flowers on her husband's tomb, which was near a church in a small village. I loved the outing and filling a pail with water to pour over the tomb, then polishing its marble and the photo of an old man. When my mother heard about this expedition, though, she went into a furious rage. I don't think I ever saw our old minder again.

I can't help feeling that the many years I was kept distant from death are reflected in the many hours I spend in touch with it now, ever close to marble tombs. I sometimes believe that in the cemeteries I frequent I'm seeking something impossible: to attend a funeral to which I wasn't invited, to be able to bury my grandmother and at last say, "What a life she had!"

On leaving the cemetery on the day of Sarah's funeral, I invited her son to follow me and do what "good Jews" do before going home: wash their hands.

The ablution separates the spaces of death and life. What the Talmud calls the impurity of cadavers is thus left behind in the cemetery.

Of course, all of this is symbolic. We actually take our dead everywhere with us: we'd know it if they stayed in the cemetery. Life and death are not hermetically separated: the cleansing water doesn't make our lives impermeable to grief.

Sometimes, I even think the opposite is true. Like washing a basket in water, our ablutions tighten the weave, and in the process strengthen our links with those who have left us. One generation to the next.

MARCELINE AND SIMONE

On Judgement Day

Marceline often described herself as a "Birkenau girl." When she used this expression, she wasn't referring to all the millions of women who had died at Auschwitz, or who, like Sarah and my grandmother, had somehow survived. I think she was invoking only certain survivors, women who seemed cut from the same cloth as her, and in particular her friend Simone.[4]

Her use of this expression always surprised me. She said the "Birkenau girls" in the way one might talk of a select club or refer to "the young things of Ménilmontant" or "the Rochefort debs." This discrepancy in registers was part of Marceline's trademark. She had chosen never to be quite where one expected, neither in word, political leaning, nor hairstyle. This last breathed rebellion.

Her bright red, disordered crop was pure irreverence: it said *merde* to the whole world—to the dogmatic, to the conservatives, and even to God. Most of all to Him, in whom she didn't believe, though that didn't stop her berating him.

She called me "my rabbi." We often told each other well-known Jewish jokes, which we both pretended to be hearing for the first time. Like this one:

---

[4] The two women in question here, Simone Veil (1927–2017) and Marceline Loridan-Ivens (1928–2018), are very well known in France. The former was a magistrate and politician who served as health minister, pushed through French contraception and abortion law, and became president of the European Parliament between 1979 and 1982 and then a member of the French Constitutional Council. The latter was a writer, screenwriter, actor, and film director.

Two concentration-camp survivors are indulging in some dark humor about the Shoah. God, who happens to be passing by, interrupts them. "How dare you make fun of this catastrophe?" And the two reply, "You weren't there: how could you possibly understand?"

Marceline was a great theologian, capable of holding forth, cigarette between her lips, on the notion of the sacred, the absence of God at Auschwitz, female orgasm, and the virtues of vodka—all in one and the same conversation.

She was also Simone's friend. The extraordinary force that bound them was not only due to their unspeakable memories of a shared hell, but also to everything that seemed to oppose them. The tight chignon of one and the savage mane of the other expressed this in almost caricatural fashion. Their political engagements and their choice of lifestyles were poles apart. For one, an absolute sense of duty, constancy, and family life; for the other, freedom in both love and politics, and the refusal to be a mother.

In the 2004 documentary film David Teboul made about Simone Veil, there's an unforgettable scene. The two women, these two opposites, are together on a bed, all but glued together, babbling and as excitedly amiable as little girls.

For me and for many of my generation, their friendship was not only a model but something of a banner. Were they aware of what they taught us?

Perhaps it's a slightly overused term, but to me Simone and Marceline embodied *resilience*. The granddaughter of mute survivors, I saw in them the possibility of taking speech back, of talking without shame, not only about what they had lived, but about the choices each of them had made. Simone and Marceline's, commitments whether in politics, cinema, or love, taught me what it meant to "stand up" and, above all, how to allow others to do so. They said: look, here's what happened to us, but remember, we aren't defined only by what happened to us. They were also somehow able, despite everything, to champion a kind of reparation of the world without leaning on the kind of competitive victimhood that sees suffering as carte blanche for outspoken rage.

It seemed to me that through these two women the story of the female condition emerged in all its complexities and dilemmas. I often told myself that one needed to be both of them at the same time—a woman of freedom and duty, and a woman who knew the power of political engagement without renouncing her autonomy.

In my mind, they sometimes argue with each other. Simone says to Marceline: "Behave yourself, do what you have to do and try to be useful." And Marceline responds: "Free yourself first of all from all these idiocies and love madly." Simone often wins the battle, but Marceline chuckles a feminist laugh and knows she hasn't had her last word yet.

I often get messages from women who have given themselves over to the one and imagine they have thus excised the other. I try to warn them, probably ineffectually—

"Don't think you can rid yourself of the twosome! No one will ever manage to shut them up."

In children's tales, a fairy godmother bends over a new-born child's crib to grant a wish or offer a talent. I've often thought that Simone was just such a fairy for the women of my generation, leaning over our cribs to whisper a potent promise. I was born in November 1974, at the very moment when her voice rang out with a solemn promise in the National Assembly.

"I want, first of all, to share with you my conviction as a woman," she said, and then went on, "I apologize for doing that in front of this assembly almost exclusively made up of men."

Once upon a time, there was a woman who challenged parliamentarians, while ostensibly apologizing to them. We know very well that she was talking to us. She was telling the girls of tomorrow that from now on none of us would have to make apologies in order to become what we wished to become. This gift, this promise of emancipation, turned us into women, free to choose the phases of our own lives, above and beyond biological dictates or injunctions to maternity.

On June 30, 2017, the day of Simone Veil's death, I remembered a very old Jewish legend. It's the little-known story of Skotzel, whose name haunts ancient narratives most often kept from girls because they are too subversive.

Skotzel was not a magical sprite but a human, almost like any other. Her legend tells that one day the women of her generation, exhausted by injustices against them, and yearning for emancipation, decided to find a spokeswoman and send her to plead their cause in person with the Eternal One.

They chose the most knowledgeable and eloquent woman in their midst, Skotzel, to be their advocate before the Almighty. All the women of the world climbed on each other's shoulders and formed a gigantic human pyramid in order to reach the sky. They placed Skotzel at its pinnacle.

Sadly, at the foot of the giant structure, someone lost her balance for an instant, and brought everyone down. Once they had all got up and confirmed that no one was injured, they discovered to their great astonishment that Skotzel had vanished.

The legend goes that, ever since then, our women's advocate is still making her case before God, but that one day she will be back, and then everything will be different. Her return will announce a new epoch of equality. And so, each time a woman comes into a room unexpectedly, she is welcomed with the words "Skotzel has arrived!" Who knows, perhaps she has finally come back with some good news.

I told Marceline this legend when Simone died. I said that

our Skotzel, our erudite and eloquent advocate, she who had argued our cause so brilliantly before the men of the National Assembly, had left to represent us in the celestial tribunal. Marceline and I agreed: the lawyers for the opposition would certainly lose their case, and Simone would be back soon to announce the news.

Simone's sons, Jean and Pierre-Francois, called me when the funeral for their mother was being organized. The national funeral would take place in the courtyard of the Invalides, and then at Montparnasse Cemetery there would be a more intimate religious service. "A Kaddish will need to be recited at my grave," their mother had said. They asked me if I would do so with them, alongside of the Chief Rabbi of France. They thought it was important for a woman's voice to accompany their prayer.

The morning of Simone Veil's funeral, Marceline and I took our places side by side in the courtyard of the Invalides. As ever, she was wearing what she called, in reference to the Hebrew for "bazaar," her *balagan* jewels: enormous necklaces and rings, and brooches in animal shapes. Life glistened everywhere on her, her bright gems and colors chasing death away. When the music burst forth and the coffin was brought in by the Republican Guard, Marceline nudged me and said proudly, "That's my pal!" In her idiom that also meant, "Fuck death!" And in mine, "*L'Chaim!*"

Jean and Pierre-Francois Veil paid magnificent homage to their mother, their words full of admiration and humor. One day, they recounted, when she had come upon one of her sons at the dinner table putting forward views that she judged misogynistic, she simply poured a pitcher of water over his head—to refresh his ideas.

The President of the Republic then began his speech. After a few minutes, the Birkenau girl asked me, "Hey, if I lit a firecracker now, do you think that would be a problem?" We exploded with laughter like schoolgirls, especially Marceline, who was, after all, much younger than me. She used to say that the age at which you face trauma is the one you stay at for the rest of your life, and since she had been arrested at the age of fifteen, the furl of her years had got stuck there. The adolescent rebel had never left her.

Around us, a few women raised their eyebrows and gave us disapproving looks. I think the Simone within each of them was speaking loudly. Marceline, as ever, pretended not to hear.

At the end of his address, Emmanuel Macron announced that Simone Veil would be buried in the Pantheon. Marceline applauded noisily. "That's wonderful for her," she said, before adding, "But I'm warning you, I don't want to be put in the Pantheon. Boring as hell there."

Later, at Montparnasse Cemetery, Marceline spoke. She told us how her friend was a "hottie," the most beautiful of the "Birkenau girls." Her charm had worked on everyone throughout her whole life. Simone's sons then recited the Kaddish, together with the two rabbis, a man and a woman, as they had wished, who pronounced the words of the ancestral prayer with them.

"*Yitgadal veyitkadash shemei rabba . . .*"

Contrary to popular belief, the Kaddish is not a prayer for the dead. It speaks neither of disappearance nor of grief. Rather, it glorifies God, singing His praises and enumerating in a long litany all the aspects of His grandeur.

"*Veyitadar veyithale veyitalal . . .*"—"He is exalted, elevated, and worthy of praise."

Like a mantra, it is made of repetitive sounds, words murmured not in Hebrew but in Aramaic.

According to legend, angels, those divine messengers, have the power to intercept our prayers and carry them to celestial spheres. They're capable of understanding everything that humans formulate, in all the languages and dialects of the world, with one exception: Aramaic. Who knows why they have mastered all tongues but not this one.

If the Aramaic prayer can't be intercepted, it's evidently because it goes straight to the Maker. This little tale, amongst many others, contributes to giving a special status to the Kaddish, rendering it almost magical.

Other Talmudic legends give it strange powers and confirm it as one of the most potent of devotional liturgies. To recite the Kaddish in memory of someone who has died contributes to the rapid ascent of their soul, propelling it to the sublime heights where reunion with the Creator will take place.

There is another more prosaic explanation for the fact that this prayer is in Aramaic. At the time of the rabbis of the Talmud, Aramaic was understood by everyone, or nearly everyone. It was important that the prayer for mourners was available to all, unassailable, part of a democratic and participatory liturgy.

Judaism has no actual clergy: everything that a rabbi accomplishes can in principle be enacted and pronounced by any other person. The rabbi is only someone whose erudition is recognized by the community and has been chosen as guide, but in no way is a rabbi the intermediary between God and humans.

Anyone can recite the Kaddish—although, according to some, there are exceptions . . .

Deep within Orthodox Judaism, some think that the recitation of the Kaddish is exclusively a male prerogative and that a woman neither can, nor should, recite it. The most conservative would still view this as a major transgression, a usurpation by a woman of a place which ought not to be hers.

That day, after having recited the Kaddish at the behest of the Veil family and at the side of the Chief Rabbi, I discovered that one of the major Jewish, Orthodox-leaning, news websites, had published, under the headline "INTOX" ("Fake News"), a breaking story: "Contrary to what the national press has declared, 'Rabbi' Horvilleur did NOT recite the Kaddish." It seemed urgent to them to put my title in scare quotes and to silence for posterity both the legitimacy of my function and the idea of such a transgression ever having taken place. There must be no precedent.

This anecdote would have raised a few smiles if it hadn't taken place on the burial day of a celebrated champion of women. To deny a woman's voice at Simone Veil's funeral was magisterially to underscore the need for her battles.

If Veil had wanted to send us this message from beyond the grave, would she have gone about it any differently? Simone Veil knew that the battle for women's rights is infinite and that none of its gains can be taken for granted. On many occasions, she demonstrated that in order to lead the struggle, you had to know when to pour water over the head of its detractors, in order not to be mistaken for one of them.

Until her death, Veil shared with us her "conviction as a woman." She did so even beyond the grave, by making the cemetery echo with a Kaddish spoken by both women and men. A prayer in the very image of her many battles.

It seems to me that even now in those no-woman's lands, those political and religious gatherings which were for a long time—and some still are—exclusively masculine, Simone Veil invites us to be daring, not to renounce anything. Her voice echoed through my journey to becoming a rabbi. It continues to do so each time the possibility or legitimacy of a woman standing where she is standing is put in doubt.

A year later, Marceline was in front of the Pantheon, waiting to see her friend heralded into its great domed premises as the nation showed its gratitude to the Birkenau girl. Not long after, in her own inimitable way, Marceline would pay her respects to Simone by pulling off a sleight of hand worthy of the most talented magician.

When a magician makes an object appear or disappear, he or she dazzles the viewers with a near perfect illusion. Abracadabra . . . Everyone knows that word, though most are probably unaware of its Aramaic origin.

In Aramaic, *abracadabra* means literally "he did" (*abra*) "as he said" (*cadabra*): it's a performative utterance, creating a reality which didn't exist before it. Through a single word, the world changes.

Judaism is acutely aware of this, as so many of its rites testify. This is most evident at the times which are solemn reminders of the power of speech to change the world, to let live and make die.

Such as Yom Kippur. At the time of Marceline's magic trick, Jews were united in large number in synagogues everywhere to mark the holiest of days: even the so-called "Yom Kippur Jews"—those who never go to prayers, who never attend synagogue during the rest of the year, gather on this date. On the Day of Atonement and forgiveness, they recite in Aramaic the words of the most famous Jewish prayer, the ultimate abracadabra, known as the Kol Nidre.

Kol nidre, vessarei, veh'arame, vekouname . . .

The ritual is always the same. A symbolic tribunal gathers at nightfall, and everyone is called upon to acknowledge their faults and ask for forgiveness. The melody of the prayer is poignant, and the words invite all Jews to recognize the vanity of their utterances and the futility of their promises. It is a public trial at which everyone pleads guilty.

On September 18, 2018, on the eve of Yom Kippur, as the words of the Kol Nidre echoed in all the synagogues and thousands of people raised their voices, Marceline decided to cock a snook at this great judicial tribunal. In a hospital room, surrounded by a few friends, she was listening to a live stream of the opening notes of the Yom Kippur tribunal. "Go and see if I'm there with the repeat offenders!" she said.

I wasn't at her side that night because I was singing the words which made all of us habitual criminals, but if I had been, I would have told her once more the story that made us laugh so much.

One Yom Kippur, the rabbi notices that, at the back of the synagogue, a lone man is behaving in an agitated manner and seems to be arguing with someone. The rabbi comes closer and says to him, "What's up? Who are you talking to?"

The man answers, "I was in conversation with the Eternal One. I said to him: 'I'm quite willing to ask for forgiveness for what I've done, but frankly I haven't done anything very terrible. Whereas, you, God . . . Look at this world, the suffering, the pain, catastrophes raining down on us. You God, you should be the one asking for forgiveness!'"

The rabbi asks, "And how did your conversation end?"

The man says, "That's simple, I said to God, 'I forgive you, you forgive me, and we're quits!'"

The rabbi fell on him violently. "What kind of idiot are you? Why did you let God off so easily?"

Like the rabbi in this story, Marceline knew very well that in Jewish tradition ample ground is given to those with cheek, or what's known in Hebrew as *chutzpah*. Even on his own judgment day, a mere mortal can hold the supreme judge accountable, charging him for his lack of compassion, not acquitting him so easily. Even on the eve of Yom Kippur, as people pray for reprieve to be granted them, another trial can be going on that puts the Divine in the dock.

I know that a lot of traditional theology is against this kind of indictment of God. Some will judge it blasphemous. They'll consider it the antithesis of the idea of a loving God whose caring ways are impenetrable to us. But this bit of impudence has a legitimate place in Jewish tradition, alongside plenty of other voices. There are many texts and stories that draw on this audacity, going so far as to put the Divine on trial for a breach of contract with humanity, ruling that we have a legitimate right to turn against Him for not helping people in danger, or for being complicit in murder.

The Birkenau girl, who had a lot of reasons for holding God to account, knew all this well. So, what better time than on the eve of Yom Kippur to do a bit of straight-talking with God, face to face, flipping on its head the summons to gather and instead calling on God to appear. When I imagine Marceline before the celestial court on the Day of Reckoning, I have the feeling that God will not get off lightly.

From now on there would be two prosecutors at the celestial tribunal of the hereafter: one making the case for the rights of women, the other the representative of a murdered people.

Some would say that neither Simone nor Marceline believed in this hereafter, and that even if it proved to exist, they would have both simply shrugged (or, according to some, lit up a joint). I don't know. But I did have reason to doubt Marceline's hardened atheism.

A few months before her death, she was hospitalized after an illness.

After a long coma, and against all medical prognoses, she came back to us. I went to visit her, along with a mutual friend, Audrey. I hadn't imagined that she would talk to us in so literal a fashion about her return to life and the way in which death hadn't wanted her.

We were sitting on her bed and had talked of a thousand things, damning common sense and its rules which prevented us from lighting up in a hospital room. As always, we laughed, and she told us she wanted to give us "an exclusive" about the details of her recent trip, which would certainly be the subject of her next book. "Can you believe it: when I was in the coma, I saw them. They came to fetch me, to take me to the land of planks."

At our skeptical looks, she added, "Simone was there too with them, and it was she who finally led me back here, telling me my moment hadn't yet come."

Her return was thus thanks to Simone. But who were "they," those chaperones, and what was it like, this "land of planks" where they had wanted to lead her?

I thought of all those tales of Jewish mysticism recounting that on the day of death someone comes to fetch us. Loved ones appear, "angels" who lead us towards an elsewhere, accompanying us on our journey out of this world. And Judaism is hardly the only tradition in which such narratives circulate.

Real or hallucinated, a paranormal phenomenon or the result of a lack of oxygen to the brain, what does it matter? Marceline knew she wasn't alone in her coma, which had almost taken her away. And, of course, amid her celestial escort there was that other "Birkenau girl," come to pay her a brief visit before bringing her back here, because her hour hadn't yet come.

Once again, death hadn't wanted Marceline.

In Jewish tradition, and more particularly in the Bible, it's said that some very rare beings can escape death, as if they were strangely immune to it.

Amongst these is a celebrated prophet named Elijah. He doesn't die, he just disappears, soaring upwards in a chariot of fire. The Torah makes no reference to his death, only to this mysterious, miraculous flight.

According to legend, this is why he can return so often to visit: he never altogether went away. Every evening during Passover, when families commemorate the escape from Egypt, he is welcomed into people's homes. The door is left open for him, and at the dinner table a cup of wine is filled for the anticipated visitor. It's also said that Elijah comes to every baby's circumcision and has done so for each generation throughout history. He's invited to be a witness to the renewal of the Covenant, to the arrival of a being who, unlike him, will one day have to die, but, before that, will be able to live.

Wherever he shows up, Elijah observes the way that despite everything, and certainly despite death, which has always prowled so close to them, Jews continue to choose life. He comes to witness this from the seat of honor reserved for him, and from here he becomes the first observer of a sacred transmission.

The day of my visit to Marceline in the hospital, it seemed to me she was heir to Elijah, inoculated like him against death and charged with a similar mission: always to be present at our sides, a witness to all the *L'Chaims* of history.

I had the feeling that she held within her an eternal ability to escape death, and that she would always manage to evade what she had so strangely named "the land of planks."

I wondered about these planks she was linking to death. Was she talking about the wood that had gone into the coffins of so many of her friends? Was she evoking Auschwitz and its cramped wooden bunks that death visited nightly?

Marceline had anticipated explaining all this in her next book. She had promised us this. But when she went off to plead her case elsewhere, she left us with the mystery, undoubtedly whispering to us as she so often had before, "Figure it out for yourselves!"

In writing this homage to her, in trying to figure out her departure, I too, feel, accompanied.

She chaperones me in a thousand ways, and I know that others have this feeling too. Over these last years, I often meet people, particularly women, who tell me how their conversations with Marceline are far from over. I don't know anyone else who has post-mortem conversations with quite so many people.

Just before writing these pages, I rang Audrey to ask her if she sometimes thought about our visit to Marceline in hospital. Like me, she had forgotten nothing of our strange conversation. After we hung up, she sent me an interview with Marceline that she had found by chance in the May 2018 issue of the women's magazine *Marie Claire*: "In the camp, where survival dictated 'everyone for themselves' behavior, there were nonetheless moments of powerful solidarity. Like the day when I was running a very high fever. Near the spot where we were digging trenches, my friends hid me in a hole covered with a plank, and there I was able to rest."

Marceline was once hidden underground in order to stay alive at a time when, above ground, death was looking for her. On the other side of a plank, in other words over a grave which would save her, a group of women kept watch. That day, thanks to them, Marceline rose again. Perhaps after that she had promised herself that, for as long as possible, she would avoid the land of planks and its terrors.

She stayed alive thanks to the women who had saved her. In turn, she saved others, telling each of them to live and to love.

All this was in our minds when, on September 21, 2018, we laid her in Montparnasse Cemetery, so that she could rest there forever.

ISAAC'S BROTHER

The Ultimate Question

They told him, "The rabbi is here, and she'd like to talk with you. You can ask her any questions you like, and she'll answer them."

I knew very well that this wasn't altogether true, and that I would have no worthwhile response to give to any of the real questions the child might want to ask. Who can offer answers to the questions that no adult would dare voice? Namely, why had his little brother died? Why had it happened to *him*? And when would his mother stop crying?

The funeral was meant to take place the next day. I knew it was urgent to tell him what would happen there, to talk to him before he was confronted with that little box in which—and he had to take our word for this—his brother Isaac lay. But what are words worth when they come from adults who have so often said, "We'll be there to protect you," and "Trust us, nothing's going to happen to you."

His parents weren't sure if they should bring him to the cemetery; did he really belong there? Perhaps it would be best to leave him at home and keep him distant from it. But all of eight years old, he was determined to be at the funeral.

Isaac's brother hadn't cried. And when I came into the living room where he was watching television, he didn't blink. He hardly looked at me. He seemed utterly focused and barely nodded when I asked whether I could sit down beside him.

The animation he was watching was called *Lego City*

Adventures. A whole world of small shapes locked into one another jumped about the screen, an animated version of what we all played with as children: squares and rectangles that connect and pull apart, that create right-angled shapes, that change heads or bodies according to our desires, that help us tell stories.

In this house, the story had been violently interrupted the previous evening. Around them the world fell apart.

Not just the world of their family and loved ones but the entire world. This is what a child's death provokes: the crumbling of a world for each one of us, the collective consciousness of an unspeakable chaos into which all of humanity plunges, in the guise of parents whose future, in a single instant, has turned into a past.

Little Isaac had ceased to breathe. And nothing anyone could say about it would begin to describe the apocalypse the family had witnessed. Slowly their apartment filled with relatives, with loved ones, with friends who tried to find the right words.

I always say to the bereaved, whatever the nature of their loss, that on top of their grief, they have to prepare themselves for a strange phenomenon: the emptiness of words and the clumsiness of those who pronounce them. The people who visit to support you as you grieve often say the wrong thing, sometimes even awful things, in an attempt to provide relief. Platitudes like "The best ones leave first," or "At least he's not suffering anymore," or "I know you'll be strong: you're not sent what you can't handle," plus any number of other attempts to make sense of the senseless—mourners have to be prepared for these.

Sometimes, paradoxically, visitors are so devastated by the loss, even if they barely knew the departed, that they end up having to be consoled by the bereaved, who now themselves cast about for words to calm these strangers. They proffer tissues for the tears of those who have come to support them;

they improvise consolation. The roles, which in reality can't be reversed, are tragically inverted.

The well-intentioned awkwardness that people offer up to those who have lost a loved one only increases when that loved one is a child. When these visitors speak, they not only have to manage their own discomfort in the face of mortality but also confront the greatest of human fears, the death of a child.

Parents who have undergone this tragedy all concur: as soon as the news hits, they realize not only that the earth has given way beneath their feet but that the earthquake has expelled them forever from a place of shelter. They are now confined to an island, cut off permanently from those spared by the tragedy. This bereavement signals that from now on you will live outside the world, outside time, in a place from which you won't return. The death of a child condemns you to exile in a land where no one can visit, apart from those to whom the same thing has happened.

Like all immigrants, you'll have to discover a new language, in which you'll babble. None of the words you know can begin to describe what you will have to live.

In French, as in most languages, there is no word to designate the person who loses a child. Losing a parent makes you an orphan, losing a spouse makes you a widow. But what do we become with a child's death? It's as if by omitting to give it a name, language has tried to distance the experience, as if by superstitious maneuver we have ensured that we won't be able to speak of it and so provoke it.

By contrast, in Hebrew, a word exists. A parent who loses a child is called *shakol*, a botanical term it is almost impossible to translate, and which refers to the branch of a vine from which the fruit has been harvested: a bereaved parent is a stalk amputated of its grain, a vine from which the fruit has been plucked. The sap flows but has nowhere to go.

Isaac's parents didn't know how to go about talking to their son. I suggested telling him in terms he could understand that words were going to fail us all.

I joined him to listen to his questions, which for the moment had been put on hold as he took refuge in *Lego City*.

Watching this animated world at his side, I wondered why the Lego universe provokes such fascination from one generation to the next. It seemed to me that these blocks and figures made a promise that life can never match: that you can attach or detach yourself without pain and whenever you want. You can break away without damaging anything, without leaving any trace either of attachments or ruptures.

When the credits came up, I turned the television off and asked him if he wanted to play or talk. He chose that moment to ask me a question, which he seemed to have prepared.

"I need to know where Isaac went. Because I don't know where to look to search for him."

I tried to understand what he meant by search. In what direction did he imagine his eyes would look to find him? It seemed to me that, like the Little Prince addressing the aviator, he was trying to evaluate my ability as an adult to depict his pain.

Then he formulated his question differently.

"I need to know where Isaac has gone. Dad and Mum don't know how to tell me. They can't decide. They say that tomorrow he'll be buried, and they also say that he's gone up into the sky. So, I don't understand: will he be in the earth or in the sky? I need to know where to look to search for him."

No one knows how to talk about death. That might be the most accurate definition we can give it. Death escapes words, precisely because it signals the end of speech. The speech of the person leaving, but also that of those who are left behind and who, in their state of shock, will always make poor use of language. In bereavement, words lose meaning. They often only serve to emphasize to what extent nothing makes sense anymore.

And so, we say, "He's gone," "He's in heaven," or "He's left us," and the child, or the linguist, or the poet—that is, all those who accord to words their often-denied power—hear lies in these utterances. Isaac's brother could hear everything that the adults were trying to veil in their words, and he asked me to translate what his parents wished to avoid saying to him.

In order not to tell children how much of a mystery death is, we end up saying anything and everything, without hearing just how our lies plunge them into disarray and reinforce their solitude. What is it that lies hidden inside everything we don't say about death? Hidden in our contradictory metaphors, in which the dead simultaneously rest under the earth and in the sky? Why do we so often refuse the Little Prince's request to draw the sheep he expects of us?

In my work as a rabbi, I've often been confronted by the impotence of language. I must make a confession here. I've sometimes been envious of some of my colleagues, in particular of those who in their theology have access to a solid and incontestable language around death. Many believers can use the language of their religious tradition to deliver reassuring certitudes. Some guarantee that your soul will travel into the heavens, that it will be "welcomed by God and the angels," or by "all the company of heaven," and "placed at the foot of the celestial throne," or "at God's right hand," in "the kingdom of the happy," or "the paradise of the martyrs." I really do envy this language of infallible dogma and ring-fenced beliefs.

As a rabbi, I'm forced to admit that my tradition doesn't offer this treasure trove of eschatological responses to dig into. Judaism has no firm views on the afterlife to offer those who worry about it. It's hard to tally up the number of times when, in a conversation about imminent death, my interlocutor has asked, "Where will I go?" and I've wanted to say, "I have no idea!"

Instead, I reply in the well-known manner of the ancient rabbinical sages. I have recourse to the ancestral art of always answering a question with another question: "What do *you* think?"

Phrased differently, my interlocutor's question is sometimes more theoretical: "What in fact does Judaism say about life after death?"

And although I'd like to answer, "Everything . . . and its opposite," most often I content myself with, "Well, it's complex," and try to sum up the ambiguous language Judaism has opted for.

So here it is.

The Torah does not talk about life after death. The figures die one by one, some of them at a very advanced age. From Noah, through all the patriarchs and their families to Methuselah, it is simply said that on the day of their deaths they rejoined their own: Isaac "was gathered to his kin" (Genesis 35:29), as was Jacob (Genesis 49:33), while David "slept with his fathers" (Kings 1: 2:10). Death simply inscribes them in the line of those who have preceded them, and they leave the world, now inhabited by those to whom they have given birth.

Biblical history is one of lives and procreation. In fact, the word for "history" in Hebrew—*toledot*—means "generations." Your life story is told above all in those to whom you have given birth.

The Torah doesn't evoke the return of the dead, nor the path which awaits them after this life. It doesn't speak of ghosts or their resurrection, of paradise or hell. It seems to distrust any excessive interest in the otherworldly. It forbids any recourse to divinatory arts or spiritualism. It opposes necromancy, embalming, and everything that it associates with the practices of Egypt, the country the Hebrews fled. There are certainly no pyramids or luxurious necropolises. The greatest figure of the Torah, Moses, has no known tombstone; no one knows where he was buried. It is impossible to gather at his grave, plant flowers around it, or make it a site of pilgrimage.

Where do the dead go? The only location to which the Torah makes explicit reference is a place called *Sheol*, to where the dead descend. Is this intended to suggest a territory or an underworld? The text doesn't explain. But the etymology of the term is eloquent. *Sheol* comes from a root that literally means "the question." You might express it like this: after our death, each of us falls into the question and leaves others without an answer. I'll let you mull on that one.

It is only much later in history that more diverse discourses emerge about the afterlife in the books of the prophets, which date to the last centuries before the common era, and, after that, the interpretations the rabbis offered in the Talmud. Whereas the Torah suggests that death is definitive, these later texts begin to embrace the idea of a resurrection by extrapolating interpretations from Bible extracts.

For example, there is the celebrated text about a prophet named Ezekiel who evokes the possibility of a collective resurrection. He imagines God opening tombs to replace the flesh on the dry bones of cadavers and bring them back to life. "I'm going to open your graves and lift you out of the graves, O My people, and bring you to the land of Israel." (Ezekiel, 37:12.)

Ezekiel makes this prophecy in a particular historic context. We are in the sixth century BCE, just after the destruction of the first temple in Jerusalem. The Hebrews are exiled in Babylon and dream of coming back to Zion and realizing a national resurrection. This metaphor of the return to life of dry bones is a political allegory. But interpreted outside this historic context, the narrative becomes supporting evidence within another theology, one that makes an eternal promise of the resurrection of the dead. The commentators read in it a redemption to come. To come when? Just after death? With the arrival of the Messiah? Views on all this diverge.

Depending on the historical context, the cultural environment, and outside influences, Jewish thought will slowly enrich its eschatological palette and its interpretation of an afterlife, grafting onto it elements of resurrection or even reincarnation, neither of which are to be found in the Torah.

The traces of history and foreign influence on Jewish thought are many, notably those of the Hellenic world. Platonic philosophy introduces the idea of division between body and soul, whereas in the Torah this dualist notion is altogether absent. In Genesis, man is created from a piece of earth into which God blows life. Existence is defined, therefore, as the junction between terrestrial matter and divine breath or spirit. When this last evaporates, dust will once more simply be dust.

Not so fast, say the sages during the Roman period. Around them, dualist thinking is developing. This makes of the soul a complete entity, capable of existing autonomously. So, the rabbis develop a discourse that borrows elements from Hellenic philosophy. They suddenly affirm that the body does indeed return to dust, but the soul returns to God, who has created it. As Ecclesiastes 12:7 notes—"And the dust returns to the ground/As it was,/And the lifebreath returns to God/Who bestowed it." Today, this verse is still pronounced at every Jewish burial.

A little later, with the destruction of the second temple, several opposing eschatological theories clash at the heart of the Jewish world. Each Jewish sect develops its own vision of the afterlife. Some, like the Sadducees, think there is nothing after death and that resurrection is impossible. Their opponents, the Pharisees, believe just the opposite, and it is they who will win the ideological battle. Their influence becomes dominant, and their belief imposes itself in the Talmud, in turn giving birth to many of the relatively normative convictions we hold today on the immortality of the soul and the resurrection of the dead with the coming of the Messiah.

Do grief-stricken mourners need history lessons? Of course not. But there is no harm in putting before them the polyphonic voices at the heart of the Jewish tradition.

These divergent voices narrate the layers of our history. The poet Yehuda Amichai once said that the Jewish people were defined neither by geography, nor genes, but by geology—"fault lines, collapse, sedimentary layers and incandescent lava."

Our identity is made up of superimposed bands, strata of the lands we have trod embedded with elements from cultures and beliefs that have influenced our rites and our ways of thinking. These bear all the remnants of our histories, of our internal battles as well as of external pressures. All this coexists and leaves traces in our rituals, prayers, and minds.

The layers can be understood by anyone who wants to listen. At each Jewish funeral, just before the reading of the Kaddish, the deceased is accompanied to the grave with the chanting of a liturgical poem, "El Male Rachamin," or "Merciful God."

At the core of this poignant text, different voices and histories, irreconcilable images, engage in a conversation that merges into an ancestral prayer. We pray that God offers repose to the departed *in this place* and at the same time that they will ultimately rest in the Garden of Eden; that their souls rejoin the sublime heights of the firmament, and at the same time stay here on earth linked to the lives of those who outlive them.

Thus, in one and the same prayer, Jews state that the dead are underground and in the sky; they are here and elsewhere; their immortal soul is united with the divine, but they only exist in our memories.

This is exactly what Isaac's parents, without knowing it, have murmured to their son. And it's to this place that Isaac's brother's question has to lead the adult who desperately tries to answer him. To search for our dead, we have to be capable of simultaneously looking in all directions, below ground and up in the sky, at the end of history and at its very beginnings.

Herein lies the Jewish inability to define a single belief, in one set of words alone, to evoke the afterlife.

For Judaism, death is precisely the impossibility of speech. It is beyond words. Thus, in talking of it, irreconcilable languages are used in acknowledgment that death can be both this and that at the same time, that it is part of a world where words have no place.

When I enter the home of the bereaved to accompany them on this impossible crossing, I know that I have only a few seconds or minutes to find a language in which I will be able to communicate with them. This will inevitably be clumsy and imperfect, but it may perhaps permit them to see the *Sheol*, the location after death, of their loved one—that is "the question" towards which this death pushes them.

"I need to know where Isaac has gone: will he be in the earth or in the sky? I need to know where to look to search for him."

Rather than answer this grieving child's question, it seemed to me I needed to tell him a story. I asked Isaac's brother if he knew the story of Isaac in the Bible, if he knew who this child was and what had happened to him. Isaac, the son of Abraham and Sarah, lived a drama like no other. He was taken by his father to the top a mountain where he was bound and almost killed.

That day, the legend says, he lived what no other son had experienced before him: death confronted him, raised a knife above his head, and was prepared to sacrifice him. Miraculously he was saved and was able to climb back down the mountain. He was alive, but not unscathed.

Later, as an adult, the Torah recounts, Isaac bore a trace of what had happened to him: a marker on his body, a reminder of what he had lived. Isaac became blind. His vision grew dim, not because of old age or illness, but, according to the sages, because his eyes had seen something that could never be recounted, and his vision was forever affected by this. No one can look death in the face without bearing the imprint of it on their eyes.

In the Bible, Isaac is not an only son. He has an elder brother called Ishmael, whose name "*Isma-el*" literally states that God is listening to him. And that is how, in this family, in the house of Abraham, the two boys should have grown up, two brothers, the one who could no longer see and the other who knew how to make himself heard.

I say "should have" because sadly in this story the two children were forever separated and grew up far from the brotherly relationship that could have been theirs. Jealousy and unspoken tension created rivalries and hatred between them, which until this day pursue their children, who fail to see and to hear each other, even less to live on the same earth. Or at least, that's what they think.

The Bible recounts that Isaac and Ishmael only met again on one single occasion and in one place—at the cemetery on the day of their father's burial. Side by side, they dug a grave to send off the man who had given birth to them.

In the Bible, Isaac lives on, without his brother and without sight.

In life, it sometimes happens that he dies and there is no miracle to save him.

But even the Isaac who dies leaves a brother in this world, and not just any brother, but a brother determined to look for him wherever he may be found, under the earth or in the sky.

I had wanted to respond differently to Isaac's brother's question, but I owed him honesty. I needed to tell him that rabbis don't have more answers than anyone else. Sometimes, they just have a few more questions.

I may not know exactly where Isaac is. But I know his family, with their eternal love, will carry on searching for him, and they will speak all the languages of a tradition which keeps alive the question that his death poses.

The next day in the cemetery, a grave was dug so that a dead child could join his forebears, and so that another child, this one very much alive, would never forget that he is and will remain an elder brother.

ARIANE

Almost Me

She makes her way down the steps of a grand stone staircase in the building where we have just dined together. She advances very slowly, leaning heavily on the arm of the man she loves. She resembles those fertility statues on which whole civilizations rest. Her stomach is enormous, her walk hesitant. I tell myself the baby will surely be born tonight.

When I think of her, it's always this image that comes into my mind.

I don't know to what extent the force that radiated from her that night convinced me to imitate her. Her daughter was born just a few days later, and mine exactly nine months after. That vision of my friend, ready to bring life into the world, certainly sparked in me the desire for the same challenge. I've often wondered whether my child wasn't conceived that very night, whether my friend's fecundity hadn't simply permeated my unconscious.

Here is how we fell pregnant, one after the other. Fell pregnant . . . but what fall? At that time, we were flying so high that nothing and no one could have brought us down.

We became mothers nine months apart, and maternity tightened the bonds of our friendship. We told ourselves our little girls would be friends forever, that we would watch them grow amidst laughter. That we would have them listen early on to our favorite musical comedies, especially those of Michel Legrand, whose melodies encapsulated the girlhood dreams we so wanted to transmit to them. These children would be almost twin sisters.

Ariane was a few years younger than me, but it often seemed to me that in her maternal prowess she was older. Everything seemed easier for her, more natural and innate. She was one of those mothers who knew how to organize and foresee the needs and schedules of a newborn. Later, she always had a biscuit with her, a change of clothes, baby wipes. She was an expert, where I was forever an amateur. There were innumerable times when I realized at the school-gates that I was alone in having forgotten to bring a snack, alone in not having checked the weather and provided rain clothes, alone in not having tissues in my bag to wipe away tears or snot.

Ariane was altogether the opposite. Never caught off guard, the duties that came with motherhood seemed light as a feather for her, part of what she had always been long before becoming a mother—that is, a truly attentive woman.

In her own way, she was the embodiment of my stereotype of a Sephardi mother. I would make fun of the way she so perfectly incarnated this cliché. She would shrug and reply that I'd be better off putting my Ashkenazi heritage and its millennia of neurotic guilt on the backburner.

Amid their mothers' somewhat cartoonish debates, our "twins" grew and blew out their first, then their second-year birthday candles a few months after one another.

One day my telephone rings. I am alone, writing in a café. It isn't Ariane on the phone, but her husband. He tells me that a routine examination has revealed "a little something" in her that will need checking, a shadow seen on a brain scan that the doctors are struggling to identify. I sense he is searching for words to downplay the situation, to not alarm me. He wants at all costs to allow for the possibility of lightness in the conversation.

But at that precise second both he and I know it: life has changed radically.

His wife and my friend have just moved house without having budged an inch. She has taken up residence in a parallel universe where the people we call patients live. In this medical realm, the holiday resorts are waiting rooms. And as for friends, they're in another world, a territory where from now on a great deal will be spoken about you, and less and less with you.

The news of an illness or the suspicion of an illness invariably produces such an effect. Of course, your loved ones continue to talk to you, but, without your knowledge, they generally start another conversation in your absence, with your husband, your wife, your closest circle. Your health becomes a subject of conversation that escapes you. You sometimes hear whispers as you approach or a conversation that stops abruptly when you come into a room. None of this is borne out of any ill-will. It's simply the main side effect of the most shared emotion in the world: fear.

During the months that followed, this fear never left us. We felt terror when the treatment didn't work, when the operation was impossible and the growth implacable, when the doctors tried to slow its progression, all the while knowing its progress was inevitable.

There was also the fear of words, the fear of what language would make us have to listen to, the fear of turning this "little something" into an object called a "tumor." Who had dared to utter this word, all the while pretending not to notice what it shouted in our ears?

Each of us may well know that we are going to die, but the fact of not knowing when or how makes all the difference. The immensity of possible outcomes makes us believe we can somehow still escape. But suddenly the tumor says to its owner: mystery over, all is revealed. It's like at the end of a game of Clue, when one of the players lays bare all the details of the crime, interrupts the play with a murderous announcement: "I accuse cancer, with its metastases, in the hospital room."

Then, too, there's the apprehension and the shame of having to recognize that we're not just afraid for the other person but also for ourselves and of the idea that the same thing could happen to us. Illness beats all of us back into the country of our fears. And Ariane's illness, because it attacked her brain, activated our most terrifying anxieties. Not only of leaving before our children, of not seeing them grow up, but of losing our faculties, of forgetting; the fear of change and of no longer being whom we once were.

Slowly the illness changed my friend, or, more precisely, it turned her both into herself and someone else, sometimes in sequence, sometimes simultaneously.

For her loved ones, she seemed to both remain the same and become different. None of us could tell whether these changes were the symptoms of the illness or her way of rebelling against it. A strange intonation, moodiness, "worrying quirks" so barely perceptible that no one knew to begin with whether these minor changes spoke of the victory of the illness or the battle she was waging against it.

The two of us often had just this conversation. She anxiously confided in me that sometimes she felt she was being split in two. The illness created this odd perception of doubling. In her mind, she heard voices that answered each other. One said: I am the one you have always been. The other immediately interrupted: Don't listen to her. She makes you believe she's you, but she's only the illness speaking inside you.

The confrontation seemed to create two opposing parts of herself, as if twin sisters were in tireless dialogue.

Listening to her describing this split, I often found myself thinking of the story of one of the heroines in the Bible, a woman called Rebecca, who, one day, in very different circumstances, suffered the agony of a doubling in herself.

Genesis tells us that Rebecca was pregnant with twins when things went badly. The pregnancy impelled contradictory forces. The Torah notes, "the children struggled in her womb." (Genesis 25:22.) Her two boys to come, Jacob and Esau, would one day embody two opposing visions of the world, two irreconcilable universes. In the womb, their combat had already begun, and Rebecca was torn apart by these conflicting forces doing battle.

It was then that she had an idea. She was the very first to go in search of the Eternal to find an answer. Before her, no human had dared summon God to ask a question of him. Rebecca did so and formulated the most powerful existential question in the entire Torah. "*Lama ze anoki*"—why do I exist? (Genesis 25:22.)

Most Bibles translate these words as the question of a woman in pain, whose womb is ruptured: what's the use of living? But biblical Hebrew, as is so often the case, is more subtle than the translations suggest.

In Hebrew, the first-person singular has two possible forms. In its most common form, "I" can be *ani*, but a more elaborate and rarer version is *anoki*. The difference between the two lies in a single letter in Hebrew script. A single consonant separates a simple "I" from its less usual form. The letter *kaf* slips into the word and surreptitiously unsettles the signifier. *Ani* becomes *anoki* by the stealth of a simple letter.

The force of this supplementary *kaf* in Hebrew is that it isn't only a letter but also a term which carries meaning. It means "almost," and adding it to a word transforms the latter into a "not altogether." To put it differently, when Rebecca formulates her existential question "*Lama ze anoki?*," she is not saying simply, "Why am I?" but more literally, "Why am I 'almost me?'"—in other words, "Why is this me who is asking the question not altogether me, but both me and someone other than me?"

This questioning, pronounced in the Bible by a matriarch pregnant with twins, in the clutches of an inner division, is the model for all existential splitting. It's a formulation that could be repeated by anyone who hears opposing voices speaking within themselves. Why is the person I thought I was suddenly speaking in a different voice? Am I also this not-altogether-me who is speaking in my name?

I often thought I was listening to Rebecca's question when Ariane spoke. She, too, seemed to be painfully engaged in a search, not for a biblical God but for each one of us, addressing to us the undertow of Rebecca's query: Why carry on living when within you there's the voice of a not-altogether-you growing like a tumor?

All of us who had been close to Ariane through the course of her illness felt something in us crack, the very echo of the split she was suffering in her own interior dialogue. As the weeks went by, we knew that we were no longer going to be totally at one within ourselves, living with the illusion of a just world or a happy end, and that soon we would no longer be whom we thought we were before death infiltrated our circle of friends.

I heard the sound of that crack very clearly within myself. It arrived one day, on Ariane's initiative and through the power of her words. I remember it well. It was an afternoon at the end of summer, and we had spent it on the balcony of her apartment. We were sitting on a rug made of synthetic grass which she had put down, our feet bare on the plastic lawn. This at least promised never to die.

Ariane asked me solemnly if, for her, I would be able to split myself and from that moment no longer simply be a friend but also become her rabbi: in other words, stay by her side during those moments which we both knew were soon approaching. I told her I would try to be both one and the other.

I have stood with the dying and their families many times. I have spoken at funerals and heard the homages paid by grieving sons and daughters, devastated parents and partners, shattered friends. Often their words have overwhelmed me.

I have often wanted to cry with them, to collapse at their sides and sob. But I always knew I should forbid myself to do this. I knew that my role protected me a little and constrained me greatly. I could envelop myself in it so as to keep a distance from the wave of emotion that carried everyone along, but which offered me, in my role as a ceremonial companion, the privilege of a floating isle that I could cling on to like a life buoy.

It also seemed to me that I needed to distance emotion, because its effects on the grieving could potentially prove disastrous. The rabbi or celebrant can't and shouldn't be in perfect empathy with those they support. There's a duty not to allow the suffering of the bereaved to become one's own; to be the steadfast pillar as the mourners collapse. The rabbi's presence in the chaos of a crumbling world needs to embody the possibility of stability, the promise of continuity.

Through her mouth and through her body, her voice, her way of standing and singing the ancestral liturgy that precedes and will survive her, the rabbi asks the bereaved to believe in a future. To represent resilience, the rabbi needs to know how not to cry, how to allow the distraught to believe in the possibility that they will pick themselves up again.

That day, Ariane asked me to put myself where I couldn't be. I should have refused, out of love for her. But out of love for her, I accepted, and I became "almost" the one I was, "almost" the one I could no longer be, "almost" the one who stood upright, "almost" the one who collapsed. I allowed these twins to settle within me, even though I knew they could only clash. One, as in the Jacques Demy musical, carried a big umbrella from Cherbourg to stand upright in the storm. The other knew that the storm would carry everything in its wake and, in Catherine Deneuve's voice, cried, "No, I'll never be able to live without you."

At each visit I made to Ariane from then on, I tried to be both of these twins, either alternatively or simultaneously. This sometimes led to comical discussions. I remember the night when we talked at length about prayer and burial, about sadness and anger, just before we re-joined a small circle of friends who had come to improvise a girls' manicure party. With our scissors, nail files, creams, and polishes, we pushed back despair along with our cuticles, chose a pretty color, added a transparent gloss to the last layer and all the while pretended that nothing in all this would be chipped away.

I remember how language slowly abandoned her; I remember the words she could no longer find and her ways of asking me with her eyes to finish certain sentences. Often, wanting to do the right thing, I was way off the mark. One day, for example, she said, "I dream of . . . I dream of . . . "

Seeing that she couldn't finish her sentence, I came to her aid: "You dream of . . . not being afraid?"

"No," she said, "of eating sushi."

We laughed at this reply, worthy of the best comedy, a cult phrase that could outlive anything, even the actors who spoke it.

Superficial tales and sacred stories flowed through us. On reflection, even our most puerile laughter formed religious moments, moments that linked us together in a profound liturgy which speaks only of eternity, like the refrains in musical comedy. And it was there that the universe started to send us signs. I don't know to what extent we invented them one by one, but what does it matter? Even this fiction brought us closer to a

God whose name we didn't need to pronounce. It was enough to choose to see miracles.

One day, almost at the end, when we knew time was limited, I proposed to her that we make a solemn pact, the kind sworn only by children in their games or combatants on the battlefield.

I said: "From now on, time doesn't matter. We won't count it the way others do. Let's decree that every hour is a millennium, and that the coming week can last a million years."

The two of us decided to refuse the concept of a deadline, to remove ourselves from the countdown that others wanted to impose, to hold on to freedom for a short time, to transform finitude into infinity.

That day we miraculously managed to modify space-time. Pulling tongues at Einstein, we reinvented the theory of relativity. Evening certainly came for those who believed in the passage of time, but not for us. Just before I left, Ariane made a sign and asked me to look at her wrist. Neither of us were able to explain why her watch, on that day, had mysteriously stopped.

A week later, that is to say several million years later, the last day of my friend's life arrived.

In a room at a hospice, we all sat around her—her husband, her parents, a few close friends. We wanted to hold her hand for a last time, kiss her lightly made-up face. She was no longer conscious, but we talked to her. We told her we were there alongside her at a time when, according to so many traditions, doors between the worlds are open. And it seemed to me that in fact thousands of people were around us: ancestors, guides from sacred texts and even those idiotic songs we liked to sing, in sparkling dresses from Jacques Demy's *Donkey Skin* musical and Michel Legrand's song "The Windmills of Your Mind," weeping Jewish mothers and the children to whom one day this moment would need to be recounted. In this room filled with silence and history, we sat for several hours, in other words, years, at the site of that most mysterious of passages. The living and the dead, those who have been and those who remain alive, were side by side. And the voice of the rabbi, that is, almost my voice, told a story to her friend.

It's the story of a woman and what she gave birth to.

"Two beings fought in her womb," but Rebecca managed to give birth. She became the mother of two boys, one of them called Jacob. This child was much more fragile and vulnerable than his twin. She thus decided to bestow on him a very special blessing: the knowledge of his fracture, the capacity to listen, like she did, to the voices of his inner struggles.

Jacob wore the name of the future, a verb that is conjugated in Hebrew in the future tense. *Jacob/Yaakov* means "he will follow," which was as good as saying that Rebecca's child was named "to be continued." His name told that history didn't stop here. And Jacob, in the image of his name, spent a good part of his life in becoming, demonstrating that he hadn't finished saying what he could still be, and thus pursuing his mother's dreams.

As an adult, Jacob, child of Rebecca, fought the length of a night against an angel, or perhaps it was against himself. No one can tell. From this confrontation, he emerged with a dislocated hip and from then on was incapable of standing straight. But the angel also left him with a present: a name other than his own, an identity which his descendants transmit until today: Israel. Jacob's other name, the name from his intimate combat, reminds him and us forever what limping means: to walk with difficulty between two paths, two names, two states, to accept being unsteady, in other words "almost" oneself.

Jacob in turn had his own children. The Torah says that at the hour of his death, all his relatives gathered around his bed to send him off.

According to legend, those who surrounded Jacob linked

the fear of this man who was preparing to leave, the agony of the dying one, to the idea that his world might disappear with him. Would those who survived him know how to carry Rebecca's blessing and forever protect the history to come?

It was then that, around the death bed of a beloved man, men and women pronounced the words that Jews of each generation still murmur at each departure:

"*Shema Israel, Adonai Eloheinu Adonai Echad.*"

"Hear, O Israel! The Lord is our God, the Lord alone."

Shema Israel—Listen Jacob, whom we also call Israel, know that the one you call God—*Adonai*—who guided your steps and the steps of your ancestors—*Eloheinu*—is also ours—*Adonai Echad*: your God and ours are one.

These words still resonate for each departing generation. They proclaim that despite all the battles waged, all these twinhoods that struggle within us, all that separates us from each other or even ourselves, there is still the possibility of unity.

This is the solemn promise that Jews make at the time of a death: to integrate something of the departed's life into their own in order to unite themselves with what they will become. They say to the dying, "Child of Israel, listen to what parts of you will carry on living within us, linked to us forever."

At the time of her passage, sobbing and in unison, we pronounced the words of the Shema Israel to the beloved woman who was taking her leave. I had the feeling at that moment that we were all standing at the foot of a great stone stairway. Step by step, we watched her ascend.

MIRIAM

The World to Come

When I was a student and an apprentice rabbi in New York, I sometimes gave Hebrew lessons in a synagogue in Manhattan. My students were mostly women, and the majority were grandmothers from the Upper East Side, their style perfect and their hair impeccable.

They came every Thursday morning to meet with me around a table in a Jewish community center on Lexington Avenue, and I imagined them easily coming together again on other mornings for bridge classes or lectures at the nearby Metropolitan Museum.

They had been studying together for years. I couldn't quite work out when they had started and how many teachers had preceded me in guiding them through the language. Their Hebrew was still at an early stage, and we didn't progress rapidly. In this desert, the Promised Land seemed far away, yet we were hardly in a hurry to get there. The weekly classes were a firm fixture in our calendars and a pleasure to prolong.

I felt that they had quickly warmed to me. They showed slightly excessive affection, garlanding me with presents and attention, and I knew that my French accent was part of the reason for their tenderness. I was their "French rabbi," and if I hadn't already been married, each one of them would undoubtedly have invited me to a Sabbath dinner at the home of a recently divorced son or would have organized a date for me with a bachelor nephew.

The American concept of a date doesn't translate well into

French. Its modalities are difficult to describe. Strict rules apply: there are things that one does and things that one must never do. Accepting a first date means one thing, but agreeing to a second implies other things.

A meeting, if qualified as a date, signals to the protagonists that the situation could take a romantic path. They've been asked to sign "seen and approved" at the foot of a document, followed by "and maybe more." American contract culture makes its way even into romance and leaves little room for improvisation.

The weekly date I had with my class of seventy-year-olds was enough for me, and the pleasure we took in it was worthy of tacit renewal of our contract.

I came to look forward to these rendezvous with my Upper East Side protectors, even if I imagined their lives in a somewhat caricatured way, almost as if they were American Jewish versions of "Les Flamandes" in Jacques Brel's song—women who dance "because they're a hundred" and want to make a show of how good things are.

My New Yorkers seemed to promote the benefits of a life clearly laid out in a standard contract, a regulated existence free from surprises and rebellions.

Amongst them there was a woman who seemed older than the others. She was called Miriam, and, at the beginning of each class, she would open her capacious bag and take out a mountain of food and drink for the whole group. She would put several Thermoses of flavored tea on the table and take time to describe each variety and its properties.

Our sages recount that, in the Bible, Miriam fulfilled precisely the same function. She crossed the desert with a starving and thirsty people, whom, miraculously, she was able to save. The biblical Miriam, it is said, had the power to carry with her a nomadic well, which prevented her people from dying of thirst.

My American Miriam too carried biblical manna, or just

about, in her seemingly bottomless handbag. She would have enabled us to survive decades of travel. And once, she even poured out one of the most extraordinary stories I have ever heard.

I had asked her whether she was as caring of others as she was of us, and she answered that she had only become this caring woman recently, only since something in her life had changed her radically.

"For years, I was trapped in a profound depression," she said. "I didn't want to do anything; I didn't desire anything. My life force had deserted me; I even stopped leaving the house or meeting anyone. Never would I have signed up for a Hebrew course. I was incapable of preparing food for myself, far less of feeding others. My children despaired and tried to give me a taste for life again. They said the things people usually say to someone who's depressed when there's no clear reason why: 'Come on, you're in good health, your children are well, your grandchildren love you. You really don't have the right to let yourself go.' All those absurd things healthy people say that totally miss the point. Depression has nothing to do with a refusal to see what's good in your life or an inability to recognize the positive sides of your existence. The knowledge that you're lucky or privileged is never what frees you from it or alleviates it. And those who urge you to come out of it usually know nothing of the death of desire. There's no hope they'll lead you back to life. They're pushing a product whose value you don't deny, but which they have never lacked. So, they have no serious sales pitch."

Miriam was witty and light-hearted. She assured me that everyone in her family shared this sense of humor. I had difficulty believing that she had borne such heaviness for so many years.

She suddenly changed her expression, and, with a little childlike smile, whispered into my ear confidentially: "At that time of my life, only one thing interested me, something that I was fascinated by. It became the only thing I focused on. Little by little, I devoted all my intellectual activity to it, my entire mental universe."

I wondered what passion Miriam was going to describe to me, what hobby she might have become infatuated with in the depths of her depression. She went on, articulating slowly, as if to manage the effect of her words.

"I became passionate about my funeral."

Miriam planned her funeral ceremony for several years. Like many, she first contracted the occasion with a funeral home, signed papers and initialed paragraphs. But what this contract foresaw didn't seem detailed enough for her. The wishes of the future deceased were noted—whether or not there would be a religious ceremony, a particular color palette for the flowers, music . . . But Miriam had many other demands. She immersed herself in writing out everything that seemed essential to her funeral rites. In New York most ceremonies are not carried out at the cemetery, which is usually too far from town. Instead, family and friends gather at a funeral home in the midst of Manhattan.

Miriam knew exactly which one would need to be called, whom the contact person was, how the hall would be arranged, and the chairs placed. She had a clear idea about the coffin in which she would be laid to rest, and of course, about the music to which she would be carried in. She knew who would come to the ceremony and where they would sit. In time she also worked out the whole musical program and which version of a piece would be performed—Gershwin by Barbara Hendricks and the Oscar Peterson trio's jazz version of Sinatra's "Learning the Blues."

She knew the size of the bouquets and their composition and had chosen which pictures of her should be placed where and how they were to be lit. Above all, she had determined who precisely would speak and for how long, and in what order the tributes would come and how they might be intercut. To her great regret, she couldn't dictate the content of the eulogies. But if she could have, she would have stipulated each turn of phrase and even written her own obituary. Of course, the press notice was also ready, as was a list of people to contact.

This obsession had often caused violent family arguments. Her children and grandchildren begged her to stop all this planning, to stop talking to them about the details of the ceremony. When they reproached her for her macabre zeal, she would say she was doing all this for them, and solely for them, so that they wouldn't have to make difficult decisions. She wanted to save them from any kind of dilemma at a time when they might be overwhelmed by emotion. All this was simply maternal devotion, pre-mortem altruism.

She tried to justify her obsession, but in her heart, she knew very well that there was something else underlying her detailed programming of an event which, by definition, she couldn't attend. Miriam had to recognize that her abulia, her lack of will and desire to live, only left her when she was organizing her own death. Only then did what the French call *envie* return to her.

In English, "envy" doesn't mean the same as the French "*envie*," a yearning which glues together *en*, "in," and *vie* "life," leaving no space for death. Miriam, in the course of her years of depression, simply became the most zealous of event organizers, the funeral equivalent of the most talented wedding planner. All that was left for her to do now was die, the one detail of this grand event which had not yet been finalized. But that was before life changed all her plans.

I have met several people who share Miriam's passion, without taking it to quite such extremes. Some felt death approaching or the strength draining from them. Others claimed to be in good shape but wanted to have a say in what death would inevitably tear away from them. All of them wanted to meet me in order to discuss their departure.

People often come to my office to talk about the ceremony they would like "to see" organized on their behalf. At one point or another in the conversation, I always have to remind them that they won't be there "to see" it.

The detailed planning of what this ceremony would be like often betrays a refusal to recognize the truth of what it is: the end of one's control over life. This attempted organization of death speaks first and above all of a refusal to accept it.

It isn't always easy for me to explain this to the person who comes to see me. I talk to them of the traditional ancient rites of Judaism. There, in principle, no place is given for all this preparation. The coffin needs to be as simple as possible, without flowers or decoration. It's emblematic of humility and speaks of the equality of everyone before death and the return to dust from which we come. In some places, in Israel for example, there isn't even a coffin, only a shroud to wrap the body in before it's deposited in the ground, and the burial happens immediately after the death is announced. Sometimes you don't even have time to learn of a death before you're told the person is already in the grave. The funeral ceremony is not subject to great planning. It answers to the demands of speed and simplicity.

It's with this same objective of humility that flowers and wreaths are generally absent from Jewish ceremonies. Death is not meant to be embellished or aestheticized in any way, and one is meant to avoid it becoming the object of fascination or attraction. The sages warn against this.

What is said in the most traditional funerals is equally codified. The rabbi or celebrant evokes the dead person almost exclusively through the liturgy, using the passage from the Torah that is the synagogue's reading for that week, or drawing on the words of a sage. The funeral oration is not a great literary creation, and, in the spirit of the entire ceremony, is entirely sober and minimalist.

These days, most Jewish funerals do not take place in strict accord with these norms. Frequently the wishes of the deceased are integrated into the ceremony: images, music, a life story, to personalize the ritual.

When I have a conversation in my office about a funeral and I confront either wishes that are very emphatic or very definite "production" choices, it's my duty to remind the person organizing the ceremony of a simple truth that the Jewish rites attempt to illustrate. This pronouncement is *a priori* trivial, but its implications are fundamental: our death doesn't belong to us any more than our body does after death. I'm not simply referring here to the time and conditions in which death takes place, but to a more basic idea and one more difficult to speak in contemporary society, where respect for the wishes of the dead is the highest of priorities.

An illustration of the tension between traditional and modern cultures lies, for instance, in the question of cremation and the dispersal of ashes in a place chosen by the deceased.

This is a practice that has spread in our societies, but for Jewish culture it is taboo, and in conservative Judaism strictly forbidden. The refusal of cremation essentially rests on the principle of respect being due to the remains of the dead. The body needs to return to the earth, and the time decomposition takes forms part of the respect owed to what envelops the soul during its earthly sojourn. Incineration is perceived as extreme violence to the dead, and the dispersal of ashes excludes the possibility of offering those left behind a gathering point, something Judaism judges necessary.

A rabbi of orthodox sensibility will refuse to officiate at a ceremony where the deceased has made the choice of a cremation. A liberal rabbi can in certain circumstances consent to the wishes of a family.

Personally, I only accept this on condition that the cremation has been part of a family discussion. I want to try to understand what has propelled the deceased to a decision which is unusual in Jewish tradition, but also how his or her near ones received that decision. What were the motivations behind it? How has the choice affected loved ones, and to what degree were they party to the choice?

I could, of course, in the name of ancestral and immutable law, refuse to officiate, but it seems to me that these very same ancient laws invite me to listen to the pain of the grieving and to stand by them. This is according to a principle I define in this way: mourning rites are there to accompany those who have died, but they are more emphatically there to accompany those left behind. The ritual needs to allow them to get through an ordeal, that of staying alive, which by definition is not in the hands of the dead.

This is another way of saying that for me there is a value greater than the wishes of the deceased: the duty of supporting those who mourn. I think the greatest respect we can pay to the dead is to consider their wishes, but to be even more concerned about the possibility of those who loved them continuing life, all the while honoring their memory with dignity.

It's the same with other wishes. Some will state before they die who should speak and who should be prevented from doing so. Some specify they want neither address, nor eulogy, nor a single word at their funeral. I sometimes surprise myself by responding with a joke that really isn't one: "What's this got to do with me? Well, what makes you think it's up to you to decide?"

This is not an abuse of rabbinical power or a desire to trample on the wishes of those who feel death is on its way. It's an attempt to invite them to recognize that their loved ones, when the time comes, may well need something else, and that the consolation we need to bring them may to a certain degree counter the wishes of the deceased. If the bereaved need words which run against the wishes of the dead, is it in the power of the latter to deprive them of such comfort?

Essentially, it's a question of accepting that the fundamental property of death is that one is no longer alive, a truism that expresses a terrifying and profound truth.

Wanting to plan one's death and funeral down to the smallest detail is often tantamount to not wanting to prepare for it. It's a way of refusing to admit what our disappearance signifies: a renunciation of control over what happens to us, an acceptance that life belongs to the living.

So, we need to respect the wishes of the dead, but also to recognize the limits of what they can impose on us, and the possibility of choosing life.

Miriam was not expecting to test this out. She thought she had planned everything. A celebrated Yiddish proverb goes: "Man plans, and God laughs." And it sometimes happens that he chooses accomplices with whom to share his laughter.

This is what he did for Miriam, on the day of her funeral.

On a hot New York midsummer afternoon, Miriam was waiting for her daughter Ruth so they could go shopping. Miriam wasn't sure this was a good idea, but Ruth had been insisting for several days now that they cross Central Park and go to the air-conditioned stores in Columbus Circle. Miriam had no desire to go out. The idea of leaving home and confronting the world seemed painful to her, and she would happily have just stayed lying down. But her daughter insisted in organizing days for her, complete with schedules and goals. She was trying to mobilize her to dress herself and put a little more make-up on than usual to mark a change. She wanted her mother to have the rosy cheeks of a woman who seems to know where she's going and will get there with a determined step.

Miriam heard a taxi hoot outside her house and recognized her daughter's signal. She went out to meet her. The taxi was in front of the door, but Ruth wasn't inside it.

"I've got the address to take you to," the driver explained.

A little exasperated, Miriam got into the yellow cab and for a moment asked herself if something might just happen to her in this heat, and what it would mean to her to die on a sun-filled day. Would fewer people make the effort to come to her funeral in the midst of a heatwave?

The taxi went crosstown on 72nd Street, but then didn't turn in the direction of the stores. Miriam didn't pose any questions. Ruth must be waiting for her at her own place on 96th Street. The car was moving north, but it stopped at 76th just in front of the Jewish Community Centre, a large glass building where her grandchildren often went for art classes or swimming lessons. Miriam was in the habit of meeting her daughter in the cafeteria of the cultural center at the front of the building. The place was cool and well air-conditioned, and she was pleased to be meeting her daughter here rather than in a crowded shopping precinct. She paid the driver and started walking towards the building.

"No, ma'am, that's not where I was told to take you. You want the building on the other side of the street."

He pointed to a red-brick building, four floors high, at the corner of 76th Street. She knew it well. On it were engraved words she had uttered on many occasions and had even written in any number of notebooks: Riverside Memorial Chapel.

The cab took off, and Miriam felt the hot wind on her face. She approached the Memorial Chapel, wondering why her daughter had decided they should meet here. She then noticed a little sign that indicated invited guests should go in. A memorial service was about to begin, and the name of the person in question was written on the sign: it was her own.

Miriam went into the funeral home's big chapel. She couldn't immediately make out the faces, but she did recognize the voice that welcomed her. It was Barbara Hendricks, and though she had heard her many times before, her voice had never carried quite this resonance. As if for the first time, she listened to "Summertime."

The chairs were set in a semi-circle, and the guests still had their backs to her, but Miriam rapidly recognized every detail of what, for years now, she had been planning. The room held several portraits of her, each well lit. There were large bouquets of roses, chrysanthemums, and lilacs, in yellow, orange, and white. Barbara was murmuring, "So hush little baby, don't you cry . . ."

But Miriam didn't cry. She hadn't immediately grasped what was happening to her. Her daughter, her son-in-law, and her grandchildren had her walk slowly forward toward a chair just for her at the center of the semi-circle. When at last she could see the faces that surrounded her, she recognized them one by one as those of old friends alongside friends of her daughter's. There were shop owners from her neighborhood, people with whom she had taken courses, a neighbor who had long moved away, her hairdresser to whom she had been faithful for over thirty years, and the doorman of her building, who must have taken a half-day off to be present.

Everyone was laughing. Then her daughter, who was facing her, began to speak.

"Mom, I know I'm taking a considerable risk in making you live this moment. But please believe it's with your best interests at heart. We've organized this day especially for you. You've been preparing for this for years, thinking over each detail of this grand event, a mega-production to which, by definition, you can't really be invited, in any case not in a way that will allow you fully to appreciate it.

"And since you talk about it to us continually, talk to your family, your children, your grandchildren, all your loved ones, who have told you repeatedly that they can't take it anymore, we decided to give you this funeral while you were alive. We thought you should live this moment that you're so obsessed by. You'll see what it looks like, and then at last, God willing, you'll move on to something else."

In the bursts of laughter from the audience and under her mother's dumbfounded gaze, Ruth handed the stage over to those whom Miriam had chosen to speak. One by one, each of the planned pieces of music was played. Over the course of an afternoon, Miriam lived her funeral.

The essential was missing, of course: death hadn't made the rendezvous. No one had put him on the guest list that day, and on 76th Street in Manhattan, life was cocking the greatest snook of all at him.

Miriam told me how funny, profound, and offbeat the speeches were. Without a coffin to constrain her, she experienced the best send-up and send-off possible. One by one, her friends and acquaintances took pleasure in teasing her about everything they would miss about her, everything they had loved and everything they were happy no longer to have to be in close contact with. They derided her cuisine and her specialties—all too salty and overcooked. They laughed at her way of lying very badly to people she didn't want to see, her art of moaning by slipping in a complaint in totally invented Yiddish, and her promises to anyone who wanted to listen that she would end up voting Republican without meaning a word of it. Never had this funeral chapel known so much madcap laughter and manifested so many signs of love to a living person.

Some will find this initiative unseemly and misplaced. Miriam could have been distraught or even collapsed at the surprise that had been concocted for her. Instead, she talked about it to me as the most extraordinary and defining thing that had ever happened to her.

She confided to me that this ceremony, which finished in tears with something of a farewell to the woman she had once been, had a mortal effect on her life, in a very literal sense. She felt something was dying in her, and it was something she could very well get by without. The rest of her life could now begin.

I only met Miriam some years after this extraordinary event; the account she gave me was undoubtedly filtered by the passage of time and the re-writing of memory that none of us can quite escape. But I can testify that the woman I met was resolutely alive and had made the thirst and hunger of others, the fundamental care the living need, an absolute priority.

I don't know if she carried on planning her funeral rites or if the idea had left her for good. I suspect she had decided to renegotiate her contract. From that moment on, she refused all the "dates" death proposed to her.

After she had told me her story, I saw my Hebrew class in an utterly new way. I understood that the apprentice rabbi I was would never again doubt the possibility of resurrection. I had been its witness.

To describe the resurrection of the dead, rabbinical tradition generally invokes two concepts, two parallel worlds: *Olam Hazeh*, the world in which we live, and *Olam Haba*, the one towards which we travel. The majority of commentators see in the second the promise of future redemption: a resurrection in Messianic times, the coming of which is still postponed. But they don't exclude the possibility that these two worlds coexist for those who might be able, during their own lifetime, to voyage from one to the other. The world, as it is, can leave a passage open towards the world as it might be. Death separates them, and sometimes it has effectively to be met in order to enter a new world.

What taste then does the *Olam Haba* have, the sages ask. Some affirm that the Sabbath contains some of its flavor, the sweetness of a time apart in which rest is possible.

Others say that the study of the Torah, that is to say the thirst for learning, offers a foretaste and prepares us for savoring it.

For me, thanks to Miriam, the "world to come" will forever bear the flavor of infused herbs. The taste was concocted in Manhattan by a woman who came back to life on a summer's day and who, ever since, offers you a glass of flavored tea, while asking the rabbi, who won't bury her, to give her a lesson in Hebrew.

The Man Who Didn't Want to Die

G iven you've supported so many dying people and spent so much of your life at the cemetery, death must no longer frighten you."

I've often heard this sentiment, articulated with less or more elegance, by people intrigued by my profession. I imagine there are others who are addressed in this way: doctors, emergency services staff, funeral-home employees.

Death would have those who are distant believe that those who see it up close have a peaceful relationship with it, a kind of serene friendliness which might even give them the strength to taunt it—"You don't scare me!"

Being religious, it's assumed, is an additional privilege: your faith acts as a powerful fear-trimmer, one that no doubt grants additional serenity and immunity against terror.

I always hesitate to disappoint my interlocutors. Should I reveal that frequently crossing paths with death changes nothing? Or should I, "out of charity," keep their belief intact and let them carry on thinking that there really does exist a way of being at peace with our mortality? Should I let them imagine that with a bit of training, or better still, according to Montaigne, "with philosophy," it is possible to "learn to die?"

Philosophers or not, many erudite people I've met are tormented by the idea of their own disappearance. I've also met just as many who never thought about death at all but were no less prepared. I don't believe that faith protects you from the fear: in any event, mine has never had that power. Accompanying the death of others hasn't stopped me fearing my own. I mistrust all those who say that dying can be learned and that there are fool-proof methods for coming to terms with it.

There are no courses nor ten-step techniques to learn how to disappear, no class nor academic program to optimize one's own dying in a single semester.

Contrary to a widely held belief, religious narratives don't necessarily permit the hero of a text to welcome death more bravely than others. Quite the opposite. Fear of death haunts many a person in these stories, and the greater the person, the more solid their attachment to life seems to be. In the Bible, the most celebrated and wisest of men, he who has seen God "face to face" and can certainly not doubt his existence, is precisely the one who refuses to die and whose fear of disappearing is most powerful.

This is the story of a man called Moses who, just like you and me, and perhaps a little more than all of us put together, doesn't want to die. The sages and Jewish commentators have chosen to recount his end in the following way.

In the Torah, the death of Moses is the subject of only a very few lines, the final ones of Deuteronomy: "So Moses the servant of the Lord died there, in the land of Moab, at the command of the Lord. He buried him in the valley in the land of Moab, near Beth-peor; and no one knows his burial place to this day. Moses was a hundred and twenty years old when he died; his eyes were undimmed and his vigor unabated." (Deuteronomy 34:5–7.)

So, the biblical hero dies at the gates of the Promised Land. He dies as all other men do, but as no other has before him. First, because no one knows where he is buried, or indeed who dug his resting place. The text says, "He buried him," but who is this "he?" Commentators affirm that God himself officiated over Moses' burial. Nowhere else in the Bible has the divine taken on such a function. Abraham was buried by his sons, and

Aaron by the dignitaries of his people. But no divine burial rites are mentioned until those of Moses.

So, Moses dies like everyone else, but also like no one else. He's a hundred and twenty and in full control of his powers. His vision is undimmed, as if old age has no hold on him and he has stayed as he always was. This figure of a hundred and twenty years became a touchstone for the Jews, the ultimate horizon, an age to be hoped for. At each birthday, referring to Moses, we say "Here's to a hundred and twenty!"—let's hope we get there; let's hope not only for the longevity of the greatest of men but also for his conditions of death.

And what do we know precisely about the circumstances of Moses' death? Of what does a man in good health, whatever his age, die? No forensic pathologist can tell us, but the commentators may have a watertight case here, and one more reliable than an autopsy: they track the cause of death to a term used in the biblical verse. Hebrew words generally carry several meanings, and for careful readers of the Bible, there is no doubt: Moses died "according to the word of the Lord" . . . but he did so in a double sense.

In Hebrew, "*al pi Adonai*" is not altogether "according to the word of the Lord" or the more modern translation "the Lord said." It can also be translated as "by the mouth of the Eternal." Hence the sages' conclusion that, in the plains of Moab, at the entrance to the Promised Land, Moses left this world kissed by God. And in this divine kiss, he gave up his soul.

The Eternal One, who in Genesis breathed life into the nostrils of the first man, Adam, takes back this breath from another man in the final lines of the Torah. He reclaims Moses' soul in the most tender way possible, and the most inspired. No one since has known this favorable treatment and left this world in a similar embrace, but everyone wishes for it.

It's clear that the sages wanted to offer Moses the sweetest of departures. But why? No doubt to soothe what perturbs all sensitive readers of the text and soften the blow of an immense injustice.

For the commentators, the death of Moses is the greatest of all injustices, and the least explicable. How dare God abandon his hero at the gates of the Promised Land, he who led the Hebrews out of Egypt and has guided them for forty years through the desert? What has Moses done to merit such a punishment?

The Torah suggests one mistake he made: he hit a rock in the desert twice to make water come out of it. Moses seems to have been reproached for this act. Should he not have hit the rock? Or done so only once? Should he have spoken to the rock, prayed, or walked past it? The interpreters argue this question, and some have gone so far as to say that the fault attributed to Moses is only an excuse: God never intended to allow him to enter the Promised Land. His journey had to stop there, and his mission found its end at the gates of a destination it wasn't his to know.

For many commentators, however, the death of Moses is unbearable. In their literature, they "invent" a rebellion for him and turn him into the archetype of a man who stands in opposition until the end, until his death.

Dozens of Jewish legends, written in different epochs, describe the fierce struggle Moses put up against his predetermined end, and all the things he did in an attempt to escape his fate. Each of them recounts in its own way what happens to a man, however exceptional and great, when his terminus is announced to him. What goes on in the mind of the person who learns death is imminent? To this question, rabbinical literature sketches responses several millennia before contemporary psychology proposes its own.

At the end of the twentieth century, numerous psychiatrists set out to describe the various mental stages a patient goes through in the terminal phase of an illness. Amongst the most famous models of end-of-life emotions are those of Elisabeth Kubler-Ross, a psychiatrist and psychoanalyst who pioneered hospice care. According to her, all patients nearing death go through the same five states, more or less. A period of denial gives way to one of rage. After this, the patient enters a time of negotiation which is closely followed by depression taking hold. Only when this lifts, does a form of acceptance of death arise.

Denial, Rage, Negotiation, Depression, and Resignation. In other words: "There must be some mistake"; "This is so unfair"; "At least let me live until this or that takes place"; "What's the point anyway?" and "I'm ready at last."

Specialists today admit that these descriptions are necessarily reductive. Each individual's trajectory in confronting death is unique. There can be no possible standardization to sum up the gamut of human emotions, no uniform model for each and every human trajectory as death looms.

But, as chance would have it, the rabbinical legends about the death of Moses, collected from the first century onwards, echo these contemporary psychological stages. They seem to illustrate, one by one, what Moses went through as he approached his own end on the plains of Moab.

In the celebrated midrash *Petirat Moshe*, or Midrash on the Death of Moses, Moses is described as refusing to believe the news he receives. God may say to him, "You won't enter the Promised Land," yet our hero continues to believe in the possibility. After all, he says to himself, didn't he already once get God to change his mind? In the desert, the Eternal One vowed to exterminate the Hebrews after they worshiped the golden calf, but Moses' intervention dissuaded Him. If God had changed His plans in the past, why shouldn't He do it again? In his denial of death, Moses seems convinced that his closeness to God will provide him with salvation or at least respite.

In another legend, Moses explodes in rage. Dying is out of the question.

So, God says to him:

"But your father and grandfather, didn't they die before you?"

"Of course," Moses replies, "but as for me, I've done such great things that I deserve to go on living."

"What about Abraham, Isaac, and those great men of past generations? Didn't they too die before you?" God asks.

"Of course," Moses snaps back, "but each of them gave birth to children who strayed. The world they left behind was very imperfect."

Moses suggests that the path he took was more exemplary and his contribution to the world unprecedented. That surely deserves some recompense. God interrupts him and reminds him of an event from his past that he pretends to have forgotten:

"Moses, didn't you kill an Egyptian?"

And the man, reminded of his guilt, sends it boomeranging back to God as he responds with astonishing impudence:

"And you, Eternal One, what did you do with all those firstborns of Egypt?"

Confronted by death, man explodes in rage and turns it against God. The commentators recognize the gesture and are prepared to have this bold human voice heard. It's a voice which does not exonerate God of His cruelties.

In another legend, bargaining and conciliation are in play. Moses proposes a deal to God and tries to negotiate a way to stay alive, despite everything. "What if I lived on in another form?" he asks. "What if I became a bird, or a hind, or a stag? I don't mind which: it could be any living species so long as I can stay in this world."

Having run out of arguments, Moses collapses, and the voice of the rabbinical legends takes up his story through an image.

One day, it is said, he drew a circle in the earth and sat down inside it, crying and screaming to anyone who might listen that his path stopped there, that he could no longer get out of it.

It's then that God put the following dilemma to him:

"I vowed two things: that I would annihilate the people in the desert after the sin of the golden calf, and that you would not enter the Promised Land. You, Moses, begged me to go back on my initial vow, and, thanks to you, I allowed the Hebrews to live. But you beg me now to annul my second vow and to let you live: so, are you prepared then for me to go back on my initial change of mind? Would you be ready to trade your survival for that of all your people?"

In this dramatic story, God acts as if He can annul only one single promise, that He has only one chance to retract a vow, and He places the responsibility of choosing which vow this will be in the hands of a man. He lets Moses choose between his own life and that of his people. The scene is cruel and profoundly immoral. But it's as if through this literary creation, this invented scenario, the rabbis recognize that Moses needed help to die, needed to be given a choice that he had to accept, unless he wanted to give up his greatness forever.

Moses will resign himself to death. His resolution to die becomes from then on, the very condition of the salvation of a whole people. Life is offered to all those who survive him, who read and comment on his story. In dying, Moses once more makes the decision to save us all.

I think the grandeur of these rabbinical tales lies not in the greatness of the hero they describe but, on the contrary, in the hero's absolute humanity. Moses may well have been a leader, a strategist, a fighter, a sage, but he remained until the end a man who knew fear and doubt, a being who, like all of us, sometimes showed bad faith and hubris, and allowed himself to be carried away by anger and despair. Confronted by death, he trembles and begs. His fear is ours, and no one asks us to do better than he has done. Heroism from then on becomes not a question of ceasing to dread the end, but of always worrying, even from the pit of our terror, about what at our death will survive us.

When Moses resigns himself to death, God asks him to climb to the top of a mountain named Nebo. From here he will be able to see the Promised Land at a distance before taking his leave of the world. The name of this mountain perhaps originates in Hebrew from a root that means "prophecy," though it could also be a borrowing from the name of the Mesopotamian god Nabu, revered in this region (now Jordan) in biblical times. Nabu was the god of knowledge and writing; his symbol was the reed pen and the tablet, the tools of written transmission.

I love the idea that the Hebrew Bible, with all its relentless struggle against idolatry and pagan deities, has its greatest hero die on a mountain dedicated to the god of writing and leaves this pagan trace in the history of the Jews, who then transmit this text to each other while meditating on death.

Amidst all the legends relating to Moses' end, the most celebrated is the one that appears in the Menachot tractate in the Talmud. This account conveys better than all the others what it was that allowed the greatest of men in the Bible to die serene and reassured at the top of the mountain he had climbed. In transmitting this story in written form, the sages ask each generation to study it afresh.

It's said that one day Moses climbed a mountain and found God at its very top, occupied in a strange activity. The Eternal One was busy drawing little marks on the letters of the Torah, as if fine branches and thorns had been placed on their summits. Still today, in all the synagogues of the world, we find these small calligraphic forms on parchments, little spiked crowns which seem to decorate the words on the scrolls of the Torah. But no one knows exactly what these tell or teach us.

When he saw God on the top of the mountain, reed pen in hand, carefully illustrating the letters of a Torah, Moses couldn't help asking:

"But why are you wasting time instead of giving men the Torah right now? What's the good of these decorative, meaningless embellishments?"

And God answered His servant:

"Know that one day, a very long time in the future, a man will arrive in the world able to interpret every little point. He'll be able to comment and provide magnificent readings about each of the little branches that I've placed here."

Moses begged God to let him meet this prodigy, to let him see who this talented man was who would arise one day. So, God created a miracle for Moses. He said to him, "Turn around."

Moses turned, and looking behind him, he was instantly transported centuries into the future, into a house of study where an extraordinary teacher, the Rabbi Akiva, illuminated for his students the meaning of each of those small calligraphic marks at the tops of the letters in the Torah. Sitting at the very back of the class, Moses listened and marveled, without understanding a word of what was being taught. What was the source of this wisdom, unknown to him, the man who had personally received the Torah on Mount Sinai from the hands of the Eternal One?

This very question was put to the Rabbi Akiva.

"From where do you get this wisdom?" one of the students in the class asked. "Who entrusted it to you?" The teacher replied with no hesitation. "This wisdom was given to Moses on Mount Sinai one day, the day of revelation, and it was he who transmitted it to us."

Moses felt assuaged. Perhaps on that day, and for the first time in his life, he became ready to contemplate death.

The agony of a man who doesn't feel worthy enough, the fear of dying before knowing: nearly everything is expressed in this text. It also reveals what might help a person to depart in peace and learn to die. Moses received the Torah on Mount Sinai, but, well after him, others would come along who were capable of interpreting what he himself didn't know. These sages knew more than he did, but they continued to say that whatever knowledge they possessed, they owed to him.

To put it another way, Moses transmitted to his people a way of knowing in the form of letters that could grow, exactly like the mysterious marks that ornament them. These branches, given to the world, would continue to develop after him. The life of Moses carried the germ that would be nurtured by those who followed him.

Each generation, because it follows a prior one, comes of age on a soil that allows it to grow that which their predecessors did not have the time to see flower.

This is the key to the transmission that God, reed pen in hand, reveals to Moses at the very top of a mountain of prophecy which bears the name of an ancient divinity of writing. God says to the greatest of men: Yes, you are going to die, but your children will manage to grow what is still only a fragile trace left by your life. The fullness of your existence and teaching remains to be revealed through those who will come after.

Understanding this, Moses is able to find a certain serenity and is prepared to accept that which so frightened him.

This legend contains almost all that Judaism can teach us about death. Is it possible to learn to die? Yes, on the condition that fear isn't denied, and that one is ready, like Moses, to turn around to see the future. For the future isn't in front of us but rather behind, in the traces of our footsteps on the soil of a mountain we have climbed. And it is in these traces that those who come after and outlive us will read that which it is too soon for us to see ourselves.

Jews affirm that we do not know what lies after death. But this can be formulated otherwise: after death, there is what we do not know. There is what hasn't yet been revealed to us, and there is what others will make of it, telling it better than we can, because we once were.

Blessed Is He Who Revives the Dead

He arrived at my place on Herzl Boulevard at the end of the afternoon, and we immediately set out for Tel Aviv. It was around six, and the roads from Jerusalem were heavy with traffic. The jams started after the very first turning on the highway. I wondered how many others were heading for the same destination as we were that evening and whether at this speed, we had any chance of getting there on time.

For several days, we'd been planning every step of this Saturday evening: the timing of our departure and the best place to park, how long the journey would be taking into account traffic, and even what time we needed to be back so that he could have a brief rest before returning the next morning to his military base.

He had authorized leave and arrived to pick me up dressed in civvies, with only a pistol discreetly tucked into his belt. We kissed and, almost without a word, set off. Once out of town, our conversation picked up. I remember reflecting that we now only spoke Hebrew with each other.

During the beginning of our story, English provided neutral terrain. It was the Switzerland of our first exchanges. Then, over the course of several months, and even heading into our third year together, we moved back and forth between languages and constructed sentences which mixed influences. Mine took on more and more Hebrew, with always a few words in French. When he left for his base, I would say to him, "Please take care of yourself, *motek sheli* (my dear)." I knew almost nothing of his daily life as a soldier, but I worried about him in all languages.

That evening, I realized that Hebrew had won out over our amorous Tower of Babel. We now spoke solely in Hebrew and probably less in general than before. Perhaps that's the fate of all couples: by speaking the same language, they end up truly understanding each other. But the end of misunderstandings can signal the end of many other things too.

After several years together, thinking we were ridding ourselves of foreign influences, we had purified our conversation. At that time in my life, I hadn't yet considered that particular lie. It took me years to understand it: to understand that no language is pure, and Hebrew perhaps a little less so than the others.

Within this language reborn out of its own ashes is a mix of voices that purport to be new or original. Yet it's a language under influence, one colonized by a painful history. Yes, it won its independence and came back to life in a modern version, but it remains a terrain occupied by the foreign realms which haunt it. Few languages, it seems to me, have as many words that come from a foreign root, grafts from origins so distant that they have forgotten they are from elsewhere.

The months of the Hebrew year are all taken from the Babylonian calendar, numerous words stem from ancient Greek or German, and even "religion," which, as everyone knows, is a heavyweight in the Middle East, is a word that doesn't exist in Hebrew. It's designated by the term *dat*, and people pretend they don't know this is a Persian word.

To speak Hebrew often comes back to detailing the civilizations with which the Jews crossed paths, recognizing the traces of what they borrowed or what was imposed on them. Tell me to where you were exiled, by whom you were ruled, who tried to kill you, and I will tell you what language you speak. So-called "pure" Hebrew is always polyglot and, above all, stratified. It is formed by accumulated layers of influence. This can, of course, be said of all languages, but the resurrection Hebrew underwent after centuries as a solely religious language makes the phenomenon here even more flagrant.

At the third turning of the main road out of Jerusalem, the terrain changes color and other sedimentations appear. The landscape is covered in small white stones, square in shape, and these are visible in their tens of thousands from far away. They are tombs.

The fast road runs along the immense cemetery of Givat Shaul, that messianic necropolis containing the remains of all those who wait impatiently for a redemption ever just around the corner. The Messiah may be a little delayed by the traffic jams on the road, but he will be there soon. He's coming, that's a promise: all the placards announce it. They bear the image of a rabbi they say is dead . . . but perhaps not.

Just as Hebrew carries the traces of many languages, the cemetery wears the imprints of multiple horizons. It's a place of reunion for the dead of numerous lands who have expressed in a multitude of languages their wish to rest here. Across the globe, people dream of being buried at the gates of a unique city, the one where the Messiah promised to make his first stop.

In their daily prayers, Jews say, "Blessed are you, oh Lord, who revives the dead." Belief in the resurrection to come puts Jerusalem at its heart, and from around the world, people come to Jerusalem to await it: according to legend, at the hour of redemption, when the tombs of those who will return to life are opened, those in Jerusalem will be first. To lie at rest in Jerusalem is to be assured that the night will be short, or at least shorter than elsewhere. And that you will be amongst the first to be woken.

I admit never having understood how Israel could be, for so many, the country where one comes to die or be buried. At that time, I understood it even less. Israel was the land where, at the start of my adult life, I had chosen to come and *live*, a country of the future and at the beginning of its history. It was precisely the place where one left cemeteries behind, certainly those of Europe, from which I couldn't quite untangle myself.

Israel was the name of both a promise and a refuge, the possibility of a new beginning. The existence of the country itself testified that resurrection is possible, not after individual death but after the collective experience of a whole people whom the nations of exile had not been able, or not wanted to save. Israel meant that this wouldn't happen again, that history from now on was in our hands. It was a question of leaving a continent of graves, and the unmarked dead too, in order to take up the challenge, the path of an ancient ancestral promise. To go towards life.

That night on the road between Jerusalem and Tel Aviv, Israel was neither a language nor a terrain for me. Instead, it had taken on the features of the man who was driving. He was a Jew of a kind I had never met before coming here. He had something complete and authentic about him with his farmer-like savvy and military haircut, a million miles from the Jewish experience of my diasporic childhood.

All the clichés that contrast a child of the diaspora with the perfect "sabra," as the Jews born in Israel are known, figured in our encounter. I was the exile, and he was securely embedded in the soil. Child of a kibbutz, he was puzzled that I knew so little about nature, while to me he seemed to be a man utterly ignorant of Jewish history and its tragedies. He was the most firmly rooted Jew I had ever met.

Despite the strangeness of his world, there was nonetheless some ancestral melody in his speech that was familiar to me. His Hebrew was sung in an accent that gave it an exotic tone, but it also had something of the messianic music that has always haunted Jewish history, that kernel of hope that has so many Jews saying, in so many different contexts, "It could all be otherwise." His seemed to be an ultra-secular version of the old song, an inheritance at once mystical and atheistic that early Zionism had instilled in him from his birth.

In their proclamation of a humanist utopia, the first Zionists had placed into a profane context the words of an ancestral religious vocabulary. Within an atheist liturgy where God had no place at all, they sang of the redemption of the earth, the reparation of the world, and the glory of a new dawn when all servitude would be ended. Their anti-religious priests revisited the eschatology of the prophets, and their writings bore echoes of the ashes of the traditional study centers of Lublin, Lodz, and elsewhere. They transposed the words of their texts onto a soil where fruit would grow, and farms would be built.

The creation of Israel was thus recounted like a biblical prophecy, by people who demanded justice and promised freedom. Their words held echoes of Isaiah and Ezekiel, bore the hope that flesh would grow back on dry bones and eyes would be turned to Zion. These legends were taken up by those not only detached from religious readings but also viscerally opposed to all the dogmatic orthodoxy that had once shored them up. So, the secular language of the renaissance of Israel bristled with the familiar sounds of ancestral messianism. But having secularized it, the founders thought they had also neutralized it.

"These are only images," they said, "allegories, myths," convinced that words aren't living things, that they only serve to speak the real, like a tool that only exists in its use. Didn't they know that language has the power to create worlds and destroy them? It's been thus since Genesis. Particularly when you speak in Hebrew.

These people no more believed in the resurrection of the

dead than they did in that of words. But here they were wrong. Because words know how to escape the grave, long before the people who may have pronounced them, and certainly before the coming of the Messiah. It may well be that in Jerusalem words are the first to waken.

I learned all this from a great man who taught the Kabbalah in this city, Gershom Scholem, an avant-garde Zionist and renowned scholar of Jewish mysticism. One day in 1926, he wrote a letter to his friend, Franz Rosenzweig. Almost a century later, we are just beginning to analyze this correspondence.

In this letter, Scholem speaks of the renaissance of the Hebrew language, which is so dear to him.

Is not this sacred language, with which we nourish our children, in fact an abyss that can't fail to open up one day? It's clear that the people here don't know what they're in the process of creating. They think they have secularized the Hebrew language, removed its apocalyptic thorn. But, of course, this isn't true. Secularizing the language is just a ready-made expression, a way of speaking. It's impossible to empty words laden with significance of their power, unless you sacrifice the language itself . . . If we transmit to our children the language that has been transmitted to us, if we, the transitional generation, revive the language of the old texts so that they once more reveal their meaning, don't we risk the possibility of seeing, one day, the religious power of this language turning violently against those who speak it? And when this explosion comes, what will be the generation that suffers its effects?[5]

In 1926, a man living in a country which isn't yet a state, but which wants to be a refuge for all threatened Jews writes to

[5] Translated from the French transcription of the letter in Stéphane Moses, *L'Ange de l'Histoire* (Paris: Le Seuil, 1992).

another man who lives in a highly organized state which is soon to methodically murder these hunted Jews. And yet it is the first man who says to the second: we must be wary of language. Listen to the ancestral violence that sleeps in words. Are we certain that lurking in them there isn't a bomb that we won't know how to deactivate?

The strongly Zionist Gershom Scholem thinks rightly that the future is where he is, and not in Germany. He knows this, but he is nonetheless ready to see the threat his place of refuge exposes him to. He affirms with humility that in saving Jews from death, his utopia might also open a Pandora's box: that of speech. As he considers the "profanation" of an ancestral, religious, and apocalyptic language, he asks whether this might set in motion an inevitable process—a return to messianic violence.

Leaving Jerusalem for Tel Aviv that evening in November 1995, speaking entirely in Hebrew with a man brought up in the language, who was secular, anti-religious, and armed, I didn't yet hear the ticking of the bomb. I was light-years away from imagining an explosion—not several generations later, but that very evening. In some two hours, a mighty detonation transformed us into "the generation that suffers its effects."

The countdown had begun much earlier. You needed only to listen to note it and hear the bursts of fire announcing its imminent arrival. We were undoubtedly playing deaf. A year and a half earlier, on the feast of Purim, a man draped in hatred and armed with a rifle had murdered twenty-nine Palestinians praying in the Cave of the Patriarchs in Hebron.

In his act, and with his submachine gun, was he attempting to wake Abraham, Isaac, and Jacob from their eternal rest so they could watch the scene? Wasn't it enough that he had already invited Esther and Mordecai, the heroes of this particular feast in the Jewish calendar, the very ones who in the Bible invoke their people to avenge themselves violently against their oppressors? A whole messianic literature joined with this holiday to propel an apocalyptic scenario. It had been written: all that remained was to act on it.

The massacre of twenty-nine Muslims at prayer by an extremist Jew was condemned in revulsion by a whole nation. Those who saluted the gesture of the killer were seen as a handful of cranks, fundamentalist rabbis who represented nothing and who lived within the pages of books it would suffice to keep firmly closed. Never mind that these works were apparently still read and interpreted in the libraries of some fanatical yeshivas—that seemed incidental.

So too did the dusty liturgies that now and again made themselves heard. Over those last weeks, old books had been opened again, ancient prayers invoked. Their words had even been spoken by rabbis in public spaces.

This time around, the words were uttered against a Jew who, in the name of the patriarchs and biblical heroes, in the names of Esther and Mordecai and all the others, had to be stopped at any cost. But here and there, too, and even in front of TV cameras, mystical prayers written in Aramaic were spoken. These, according to the extremists, had the power to kill. According to legend, they could provoke the death of the one against whom they were directed.

"Well, if that's all," we said to each other, shrugging in disdain as we listened to them mumble. Since when do words kill? What power can these cranks have against the democratic force of a powerful and well-organized nation?

But the words were now being pronounced against a man called Yitzhak Rabin, the prime minister of the State of Israel, the very man with whom we had a rendezvous that evening.

We made our way into Tel Aviv. There were a lot of people. It was impossible to drive to the spot where the demonstration was taking place. We parked further away than we had foreseen, and we followed the movement of the crowd into the maze of the white city. In Ben Yehuda Street, named for the man who had revived Hebrew, the first placards appeared. On Boulevard Arlosoroff, named for the man who had been killed there one night, the crowd grew dense. In Ha-Kalir Street, named for the great sixth-century liturgical poet whose verses are still sung, stickers were being distributed. On this route of the dead still vivid in memory, we started to hear the massed voices of the demonstrators.

"The people want peace," they shouted, and we all took up the slogans. We knew very well, as people do everywhere in the world even when they act in minimal good faith, that when a slogan starts with the words "The people want . . . " or "The people think . . . " or "The people say . . . " a partial lie is being uttered. If "the people" all spoke in one voice or aspired to unity, the protestors wouldn't be here chanting at the top of their lungs to another sector of "the people."

We threaded our way through the main square, then still named the Kings of Israel Square. Soon the kings would disappear from the square, and it would bear the name of the man we were waiting for. But at that time, no one could imagine what would happen next.

Perhaps a specialist in Jewish thought could have alerted us. After all, in the Bible, kings never reach old age, and kingdoms are dismembered. They collapse into violence and give way to chaos. One of the kings, purportedly Solomon, declared in Ecclesiastes: "Vanity of vanities, all is vanity," and a little later in the same text underscored the evanescence of dreams, empires, and loves. Solomon knew very well that nothing endures, but did he imagine that one day his adage would be applied to a place that commemorates the kingdoms of Israel? It, too, would fall.

We made our way across Kings Square to join the people waiting for us. They were soldiers in my boyfriend's unit who more or less shared our convictions, old friends of his, well used to these leftist peace rallies. We sang, then listened to some speeches.

At last Rabin made his way onto the stage, and the enormous crowd grew silent to listen to him. I remember his words. I think they were imprinted on me because I heard them as I stood beside young soldiers who spoke of peace with guns in their belts. And I, who wasn't and would never be a soldier, suddenly felt I was attending a high-level briefing for superior officers preparing a perilous mission.

Rabin said, "I served in the army for twenty-seven years. I fought for as long as there seemed to be no chance of peace. Today I am convinced that peace has a chance, a great chance."

And then we heard him sing. It's a song that has become famous because it was his last. Repeated a thousand times since, this hymn sees the dead speak. A strange premonition.

This "Song of Peace" affirms that those who have departed can address those who still live and say to them, don't try to wake us; far better to let peace come, and live.

Rabin sang with a touching clumsiness: *Mi asher kava ner o . . .*

> He whose light has gone out
> And who is buried in the dust,
> No cry will awaken him
> Or bring him back
>
> No one will resuscitate us
> Or bring us out of a darkened pit.
> Neither the cheers of victory
> Nor songs of praise will do it
>
> Just make peace come
> And shout the song of its arrival.

Rabin's final song affirms that what is dead is dead and there is no time to be wasted in a project of resurrection. The times are not about resuscitating the dead but about waking the living. It also underlines the uselessness of prayers and the vanity of national pride.

A few minutes before his death, Rabin couldn't know that the popular song he had chosen to sing refuted, point by point, the theology of his assassin; nor could he know the ultra-nationalistic messianic fervor of his shooter. Time was running out. But at the end of his singing, Rabin was still alive. We left the square quickly to avoid the crowds and their dispersal.

Everything seemed normal, very calm. We took the route out of Tel Aviv that leads toward Jerusalem. Traffic was moving. We turned off where the road divides towards the Galuyot Kibbutz, the slip road bearing a name in Hebrew that means "The Rallying Point of the Exiles."

I don't know whether it was the road sign that sparked my reflections, but I remember then thinking about my own exile and what, in this country that I liked so much, nevertheless remained forever foreign to me. I thought of the young people with whom I had been this evening, of our varied backgrounds which would never coalesce in a unity. The people might want peace, but each one of them also wanted something else. Does one ever reach the end of one's solitude?

I also thought that I was no longer sure whether I loved the man beside me. The world we had built together over these last three years could send each of us back into exile. We needed to stop saying "we" and agree to find again what had once made each of us a stranger to the other. Our lives had taken on a settled nature, and the habitual had made us forget the very foreignness that had once permitted us to love one another.

We drove in silence, peacefully. Peace is sometimes suffocating when it silently foreshadows the storm to come.

When the hills of Jerusalem appeared on the horizon and the road started to climb, our ears, as ever felt a little blocked. I swallowed hard, and he turned on the radio. The explosion its speech brought blew away everything in its passage. I wanted never to hear anything again.

The detonation bore the voice of a man: Eitan Haber, the prime minister's spokesman. Four Hebrew words reached my still somewhat blocked ear: "*Memshelet Israel modia betadhema . . .* "

"The Israeli government announces with shock . . . " the death of its prime minister. The voice was buried in shouts. We stopped the car on the side of the road near a village called Motza, and it's there, for me, that Yitzhak Rabin died. Not on a square in Tel Aviv, nor in the hospital he was rushed to, but on a Jerusalem hill at the edge of a village. My dream stopped breathing, and with it, my love. My Zionism found itself in an impasse, at a dead end.

At Motza, I abandoned a dream in the way one puts down a suitcase, all the while asking oneself what it is that has made it so unbearably heavy. I questioned what I had invested in this love of mine and in this utopia, in this journey that had led me so far from where I was born.

I had seen in it what preceding generations had transmitted to me—languages intermingled with the aborted projects of those who had given me life, the residues of broken hopes that I wanted to repair, and everything that I had attempted to flee. It was tantamount to the end of a love story when you suddenly see the cracks you wanted the other person to fill in, recognize the illusions that allowed you to love. Now my eyes had opened on another reality. I saw, through Rabin's death, that my Zionist and amorous confusions were one and the same.

I don't exactly remember what happened next, after the tears and sobs that choked us, the sleepless nights, the knots in our stomachs, the Israeli government and its shock.

The next thing that looms large in my memory was the day of Rabin's funeral. The entire world seemed to have gathered to come and bury the man and slip a peace process into his coffin. The traffic in Jerusalem stopped. All the streets were blocked off to permit the official convoys to cross the city. From the windows of my apartment, I had prize seats from which to watch the cars of the various heads of state rolling by and try to guess which countries, one by one, had come to present their condolences.

The ceremony took place at the end of Herzl Boulevard where I lived, at the cemetery also named after the father of Zionism who rests there. I'm not sure that Herzl would have appreciated that the Jerusalem street that commemorates his history and project leads directly to graves. Next to Herzl's tomb lie all the heads of government and presidents of Israel, all those, too, who found their eternal resting place here and who of course must await the coming of a Messiah they don't believe in, who will awaken them. What will they say to him when they discover what has been created out of their dream?

Some twenty-five years have gone by since Rabin's assassination. A short while after that November night, I left my man, and a little later, the country too. I learned to live with the sorrow of this early lost love.

But I never stopped being a Zionist, although I realized that, for me, ever since that night the word itself had died a little, as though lost in translation. Try to clarify it, and the meaning vanishes to be incarnated elsewhere.

That night of November 1995, I understood that my Zionism and that of Rabin's assassin had so little to do with one another that they really couldn't carry on wearing the same name, but I had no other one to propose.

Rabin was assassinated by proprietorial Zionism, a messianic nationalism which sees in land the sign of the promised redemption. In the eyes of the killer, it was necessary, above all, to prevent a man giving others land which purportedly belongs to the Jews forever. Even at the cost of peace, none of this territory could be lost, because God had attributed it to us through the intermediary of text. And to return these lands would be against His will.

A supreme paradox: to keep this territory, it was necessary to assassinate the man who, as chief of staff, had placed it within Israel's authority in the Six-Day War of 1967. This war, and the wind of messianism it set blowing raised a generation of landowners who, by 1995, considered themselves old enough to manage their inheritance.

This Zionism, which isn't mine, invokes an ancestral promise to keep itself alive, an inalienable right to property and the force of a biblical land registry. "Go in and possess the land which the Lord swore to your fathers—to Abraham, Isaac, and Jacob," they quote repeatedly in order to reassure themselves of their entitlement.

My attachment to Israel is diametrically opposed to this land-owning, proprietorial mentality. And yet it seems to me that it is nonetheless equally nourished by biblical promises and prophetic ideals. It feeds on other biblical texts, notably all those in which God tells the Hebrews not to pay homage to Baal, the pagan god of property, not to worship false gods. Remember that "your offspring shall be strangers in a land not theirs," God says, and just like Abraham, that we are "strangers" charged with putting in place justice and equality. And it is these, not ownership, that creates the legitimacy of our stay.

My Zionism is forever nourished by exile, by *not* belonging, by the knowledge of everything that this land, like this language, owes to its encounter with others, with the strangeness that shapes it and continues to speak through it.

The absolute legitimacy of a people to live and build in a land comes from the memory of the Jewish condition, to which the diaspora, through so many centuries, bore witness. Remember that you were a slave in Egypt; remember that your father was a wandering Aramaean; remember your own past history worshipping idols—these are all injunctions the Bible gives the Hebrews who will settle in the Promised Land. It tells them never to forget what they owe to their origin, which isn't here but elsewhere. Don't imagine that this land is the land of your birth. It is not a fatherland in the etymological sense: your fathers were not born there; rather, it is a place which will ensure you don't forget where you have come from. With the memory of exile intact, this land will teach you to love an Other who you will agree to never fully understand or possess.

There is a Zionism that is a conviction of the settled. There is another, which, like a nomad's prayer, dreams of offering a place of refuge to strangers. The first kind is no more "diabolic" than any other of the world's nationalisms, though it displeases those who make of it the object of an obsessional hatred. With Rabin, the second kind of Zionism perhaps died. Or perhaps, from the start, it never had a real chance of existing. But when I think of this Zionism and the dream it carried, it makes me want more than ever to believe in that ancestral Jewish notion of the resurrection of the dead. I want to hope that there exists a possible return to life for humans, for their loves, or for their ideas. I would so like, in my lifetime, to be there for that.

Twenty-five years have passed since the death of Rabin, and contrary to everything I could have imagined back then, I became a rabbi, a word which in its feminine form in French, *rabbine*, echoes the name of Rabin. The pun makes me smile, almost as much as the unforeseeable twists in the plotlines of life.

Twenty-five years later, I watch my children grow up in France, yet I hear my son speaking to me in a language I recognize, the language that has borrowed from so many others and holds in itself layers of history. He talks to me about Israel and his wish to go to live there one day. I listen to him in silence. I smile, thinking of a lost love whose traces he has recovered, of a dream, almost dead, which has somehow survived in him, of the way in which what we believe to be almost gone can be reborn elsewhere. Blessed are you, oh Lord, who revives the dead.

EDGAR

Am I My Uncle's Keeper?

A ditch was dug, and Cain said, "That'll do!"
Alone he descended into the somber pit.
But once he had slipped into his shadowy seat
And the door was sealed on the tomb,
The eye was there, staring across the room.
Translated from Victor Hugo, "La Conscience"

Like many school children, I recited this poem of Victor Hugo's at an age when I was still incapable of understanding it. Instinctively, though, it terrified me. It still plays in my inner ear when I visit cemeteries. I think of those who murmured the lines before me and who rest in their tombs. I imagine what they built and left on the earth—cities and walls, towers and tunnels, children and hopes—before going down into the dark, and, like Cain, confronting that eye of conscience.

Few poems describe so powerfully what conscience is, especially guilty conscience, the one that leads people to feel themselves spied upon in all circumstances, wherever they go, even as far as the grave. This all-seeing, persecuting eye offers no respite, no place of asylum.

Schools still teach this poem, but few are the children who, in reciting it, recognize the details of the biblical story where its inspiration lies. In the first sections of Genesis, contrary to Hugo's poem, it's not an eye pursuing the murderer but rather a mouth denouncing him from beyond the grave.

The Bible begins with a fratricidal story. It tells of the birth and history of the first children in the world, the sons of Adam and Eve.

In giving birth to her eldest, Eve declares: "I have gained a male child with the help of the God." (Genesis 4:1.) This is why she names her child "Cain," a name that signifies acquisition or possession. No sooner has he seen the light of day than the first child in the world is "possessed"—by a mother, by God, by a name that determines his life. Very quickly he develops a landowner's instinct and becomes a farmer. He is the man who plants, puts down roots, and makes the earth fruitful. Cain will later give birth to considerable progeny, who in their turn will take root in many places. Genesis describes his sons as a succession of builders, citizens of multiple talents, who become masters of craft and metal work, who manipulate solid materials that can endure without eroding. His children found cities and settle down in order to acquire and transmit. Cain's world is built to last, unlike that of the brother who is born alongside him.

Just after the birth of her eldest, Eve has another son, one she seems to hold in low regard. She calls him Abel—or Havel in Hebrew. Literally this means an evanescent breath, or simply vapor. So, the youngest is designated "ephemeral," and from his very arrival seems to just be passing through. He becomes a shepherd of small flocks, in other words a nomad. Abel doesn't settle anywhere and has no property. He walks with no destination and has no anchor. He takes a few beasts to pasture, then moves out of history as quickly as he has entered it, killed by his brother.

The circumstances of the murder are made precise in the Bible: the two brothers make an offering to the Eternal One, but divine attention is accorded only to Abel and refused to Cain. How can this be tolerated? Why should one brother have a privilege not accorded to the other? Envy and resentment drive Cain to his crime; in Hebrew the word "envy," *Kina*, is a derivation of the name Cain (Kain). Only the one who lives to acquire can envy another to the point of destroying him.

Abel dies and disappears without a trace. He seems to evaporate like his name, but, in reality, he endures elsewhere. His voice calls the reader from the very depths of the text.

"Where is your brother Abel?" God asks the assassin right after the murder.

"I do not know. Am I my brother's keeper?" Cain replies, with all the aplomb of someone who is gagging his conscience and fleeing responsibility.

"What have you done?" the Lord persists. "Your brother's blood cries out to Me from the ground." (Genesis 4:9–10.)

The disappearance of Abel leaves an audible trace: the verse shouts it out. Abel's voice howls from the grave, and God hears it. The Jewish commentators prick up their ears at the passage, too, noticing a detail in the text, an unusual formulation. In the original Hebrew, the voice that howls from the depths is that of Abel's "bloods" in the plural. Did Abel, they ask, have several bloodlines?

The rabbinical commentators offer a transgenerational interpretation of this detail. From the grave, all the generations that would have stemmed from Abel howl at God. Cain has not simply murdered one man but also all of his potential successors, all those who might have come into the world through him. With Abel, many die, many who could have been. In Victor Hugo, these howling voices take on the form of an eye in the tomb. In the Bible they escape the earth and pursue Cain. They are the call of his conscience that even death won't silence. Above and beyond his single life, the voices ask each of his descendants, that is, all of us, to confront the vaporous welter of past existences, of all that might have been and which, precisely because it never came to pass, has left its imprint on us.

The confrontation of Cain and Abel in Genesis is thus not simply the murderous rivalry of two brothers. Through them, ranked against each other in each generation, forever, are two opposing forces: what endures and what passes; what we want to be permanent and what we know is ephemeral; "it is" and "it could have been."

Each visit to the cemetery takes us back to the genesis of this story. To whomever opens an eye or lends an ear, it poses these same questions: what traces have the departed left in our lives? What do we carry within ourselves of what they did, or on the contrary, didn't manage to do? What will we, in our turn, leave behind on this earth, which we are only passing through? There is no need to be a murderer to understand Cain's anguish: it's the fear of renouncing gains and the terror of knowing one's own impermanence.

I was very young when I first saw an eye staring at me. Wherever I went, it looked straight at me. Whatever I did to escape it, it was always there. This eye was on a canvas, hanging on my grandparents' dining-room wall. On this large painting, altogether huge to the little girl I was, a man stood upright. He was called Edgar, and everyone called him "Uncle Edgar."

I knew nothing about him except that he had died not long before I was born. He had been a doctor: the painting showed him in a white medical coat, an old-fashioned stethoscope in his hand. When I was a child, my curiosity grew more acute every time his name was spoken. The adults always talked of him in the same way. They would evoke his originality, his rebellious spirit, and suggest, without actually saying it, that he had been a great seducer. Had he seduced the artist or the patron of this canvas? Had he himself commissioned it? Did he love his image so much that he wanted it to be larger than life? I don't know.

What perturbed the little girl who looked at the portrait was above all the manner of representation the artist had chosen. Like the famous Mona Lisa, Uncle Edgar had been fashioned in such a way that his eyes followed you wherever you were in the room.

No matter where I went, and I tried this out many times, no corner of the room protected me from his penetrating gaze. For a while, I didn't go into my grandparents' dining room on my own. Like Cain, I was looking for shelter from the eye. But at mealtimes, the eye always found me.

Years later, it even left that wall to pursue me elsewhere. When my grandparents died, my father decided to put the painting up at our place, and from then on there was no escape at all. Until I left my parent's house, I saw Edgar every day, and every day he saw me. I eventually learned to return his gaze, without fear, and I ended up knowing every detail of his face. In the painting, he must have been around forty, more or less the age I am now. The color of his skin was surprisingly pale, almost cadaverous.

I recently read that in the nineteenth century it was very common to photograph or reproduce the likeness of loved ones after their death. No sooner had a person breathed their last than an artist was called to photograph them and thus preserve the image of their features, fixed by death. Some artists went so far as to stage the corpse: sitting on a sofa, leaning on a cupboard, in the arms of a family member, or even reading. These days, such a funereal *mise en scène* would seem out of place. We no longer, or rarely, look at the faces of the dead.

Jewish tradition prohibits it altogether. It demands that the face of the departed remain covered: it's unthinkable to observe a person who cannot look back at you. Other religious traditions encourage a last look at the face of the deceased. But this is not usually the image people seek to immortalize. Preferred are the pictures taken while they were still fully alive.

I often think of all this when I'm in cemeteries and see those small oval pictures set into the stone of the tomb. I wonder why this photo and not another was chosen. When people die at an advanced age, who decides to fix in marble an image of them at the age of ninety rather than at thirty? And how could a single photo convey a life when it freezes it for eternity into a single moment?

Should one evoke the deceased with a face in maturity, or with a photo of a chubby-cheeked baby or an adolescent? What age would we like to be forever in the traces we leave for those who survive us?

In his pale-skinned portrait, Edgar is very much alive and in his prime. He would only die several decades later, to be buried in a small Jewish cemetery in Alsace on the land where his family—my family—came from.

As for me, born when he was no longer alive, I seemed to intuit very young that this painting was a bridge between our two eras and told a piece of history that had evaporated. It was this that was staring me right in the face.

The story of the Jews of Alsace-Lorraine is not easy to retrace. It is a region of complex identities as a result of shifting borders that turned those who lived there, even those who were permanently settled, into nomads. As borders were redrawn, men and women who had never left their homes were transformed into foreigners. The culture of Alsace-Lorraine is caught between two worlds, even more so for its Jews. In France and elsewhere, Jews were long known as "Israelites," a designation that seemed to "sound better" than Jews. One day they found refuge in the Alsace countryside and settled here, between cities and languages. They mixed German, Alsatian, Judo-Alsatian, and Hebrew with their passionate love of France and the French. They grew up between several cultures, aware that borders, like identities, are more of a moveable feast than people say. In Alsace they established a world now almost wholly gone: one of rural Jews in the east of France.

The image of the cosmopolitan nomad has been attributed to Jews throughout their history. One imagines them ever en route, wandering from town to town, waiting for expulsion. This notion of the wandering Jew has buried the other forms of Jewishness that history has seen: ones that are rural and rooted.

The Jews of Alsace-Lorraine owned no land. They were forbidden from being property holders. Nonetheless, in the villages where they settled, they were invited to take on a certain number of traditional trades: animal merchants, teachers, shopkeepers, and more rarely doctors.

They mostly got on well with the local peasants, and traces of this relatively successful cohabitation survive today in the form of synagogues, schools, and cemeteries. The area held fertile Jewish life, rooted in the countryside, a kind of "Israelite" ruralness.

For centuries, this unsung identity created a peaceful enough dialogue between the voices of Cain and Abel in the countryside of Alsace-Lorraine. Like Abel, these non-landowners were in charge of various kinds of livestock, but they worked hand in hand with those who planted and cultivated. They allied themselves to a Cain who wasn't intent on murdering them, so they thought themselves solidly settled. Then one day, the sons of Cain once more hunted down their brothers, and, like the biblical Abel, these brothers had to disappear without a trace, to evaporate from the region they had so loved. After the war, after the exodus and deportation, very few of the survivors chose to settle here again. Their descendants didn't return either.

I would undoubtedly never have gone back, if, while writing this book, a certain event hadn't lured me there. You could say that the voice of the blood of my ancestors suddenly called to me from the soil of Alsace.

On December 3, 2019, the Jewish Cemetery of Westhoffen was desecrated. Some hundred gravestones were graffitied with swastikas; stelae were overturned. The perpetrators were never arrested. But the same people, or others of their ilk, had already targeted other Jewish cemeteries in the region.

I learned on that day that the cemetery in Westhoffen was where my family was buried, and that the village was the one where for generations my paternal relatives had lived and died. In that cemetery, where I had never set foot, my Uncle Edgar lay buried.

Suddenly the man whose gaze I had fled for years came back into my life. I knew immediately that I would have to go to his grave and make sure that his stone was upright and unharmed, so that he could close those eyes and rest in peace.

On the way to Westhoffen, the name of a Jewish woman, Ruth Halimi, kept echoing in my mind. She was a dignified and immensely courageous mother. I remembered her face and above all her words. After the atrocity of the anti-Semitic assassination of her son, Ilan, by a barbarous gang, back in 2006, and after he had been buried in a Paris suburb, she made the decision to have his body exhumed and transported for burial to Jerusalem, where he has rested ever since. Questioned about her decision by those who didn't understand, she replied that she couldn't bear the possibility of her son's burial place being defiled. She feared that, on top of his murder, some would seek to do him further harm. She hoped that in Israel her son would not suffer further.

The follow-up to her story proved her right. The commemorative markers placed for Ilan Halimi were regularly the object of attacks, and until this day, trees planted in his memory are frequently pulled up. Anti-Semitic hatred targets Jews while they are alive and persists even after their death. It is as if nothing could expunge the hatred, not even the death of the body. Does the anti-Semite also hear the blood of his brothers howling from the ground? Does he imagine he can silence it by attacking the dead?

I walked for hours in the streets of Westhoffen. Something felt familiar, although I'd be hard put to say quite what it was.

Perhaps it was the color of the stone or the scent of the vines. At the end of a narrow street, I found the big synagogue, deserted, emptied of its benches, its ritual objects, and, of course, its congregation. But something at the heart of this absence spoke to me less of emptiness than of the traces that persist.

In the small streets at the center of the village, I discovered that almost each door bore one of these traces. It took the form of transversal notches etched in the stone or wooden doorposts of the houses. Of course, I knew what these marks meant. At one time a *mezuzah* had hung there, an often ornate little box containing a parchment inscribed with verses from the Torah that Jews always hang at the entrance to their homes. The holes and marks around these village street doors told of the people who had once lived here. Like the *mezuzot* at their doors, they had once been firm fixtures here; then one day they had disappeared. Nothing remained of them now apart from an absence engraved on each house, the trace of a disappearance. What is fleeting can leave indelible prints.

In Jewish tradition, in order to inhabit a place, you have to hang a *mezuzah* there, of course, and this little box reminds us of the importance of doors and passages in our lives. But in theory you also have to ensure that the house meets a second criterion. Since the destruction of the Temple of Jerusalem, all homes need to remain unfinished. Jewish tradition would have it that a small crack or an unpainted section is left on a wall, or a small tile kept missing from the corner of the floor. Our lives need to bear a trace of incompleteness. We need to know how to live in a house where lack has its place. We need to be able to recognize the traces left by what has gone and hear it say to us, remember those who are no longer here.

I pushed open the gate of the "Israelite" cemetery, at the end of the main road. The hinges were rusty, and I had to push very hard, as if the dead, in order to better protect themselves, had found a means of barring access to the living. I started to search for the graves of my ancestors, but before finding them, I discovered that they were in excellent company.

In this tiny Alsatian village, the forebears of illustrious families are buried. The ancestors of Karl Marx, Leon Blum, and Robert Debré; of the Chief Rabbi Guggenheim, the mathematician Laurent Schwartz, the journalist Anne Sinclair.

The little Jewish cemetery of Westhoffen turns out to be something of a deceased *Who's Who* of the great Franco-Jewish dynasties. It's as if this little village had for a while welcomed and nourished the seeds of trees, which blew away to grow and fertilize the land and spirits of the world, to fight for the Republic, to engage in science, medicine, communism, and religious thought. On these very few square kilometers, the roots of men and women who migrated elsewhere had been planted. Sometimes they traveled a great distance. They tried in their own way to be their "brother's keeper." But on their respective journeys, what did they really carry of the Westhoffen soil? And what did they leave behind of their history?

To describe what I felt in that cemetery, a word coined by an Australian philosopher in the early years of this century comes into my mind: solastalgia. It's a very particular form of nostalgia for the place one finds oneself in while knowing it no longer exists, that what has been is gone. Yet the traces of this vanished world preserve its secret as palpably as if it were unscathed.

I finally found Edgar's grave and his stele, posed right next to his parents, my own great-great-grandparents. I silently recited a Kaddish, counting the absent as among my phantom *minyan*, a virtual quorum.

At the beginning of history, the Bible tells us, a man killed his brother. His act of violence set up a howl that resonates to the end of time. It drives Cains in every generation to rise up and reproduce his act. There's a recurring desire, it seems, to be rid of the Abels, to wipe out those who remind us that nothing lasts, that we have to learn to live with lack and be prepared to renounce everything we've acquired.

The man in the Bible who elaborates this better than all others is Solomon, King of Jerusalem. Solomon is above all a man of possessions. Throughout his life, he amasses goods, riches, money, and women. He builds palaces, plants trees, harvests fruit, accumulates treasure. He is a man of considerable and tangible power, in the tradition of the sons of Cain.

At the end of his life, he writes a book called Ecclesiastes, a document in which he repeats that phrase known to all: "Utter futility. All is futile!" It's one of the most famous verses of the Bible. It is also one of the most poorly translated.

In Hebrew, Solomon states it thus: "*Havel Havalim Hakol Havel.*" Here, the King of Jerusalem is not talking of futility, but is saying literally, "Vapor of vapors; everything is vapor." Or even more simply, "Abel of Abels . . . all is Abel!"

Thus speaks the sage, the landowner, the sedentary man who has acquired goods and believed in the stability of the world. Now he recognizes that all is Abel, Havel, mere evanescence. Everything that we build solidly ends up wearing out, disappearing, while that which is fragile, ephemeral, fallible, paradoxically leaves indelible traces in the world. The mists of past lives don't evaporate: they permeate us and lead us where we never thought we would go.

Bent over Uncle Edgar's tomb, an Abel amongst so many others, I closed my eyes. When I opened them again, I suddenly saw the contours of this little village with its particular history. On the heights, above the cemetery, as far as the eye could see, there were orchards. Westhoffen: World Capital of the Alsatian Cherry—I now remembered the sign on entering the village.

Suddenly an intense sweet taste pervaded my mouth. It seemed to act as confirmation. My roots, like those of the cherry trees, lay here. Stupidity, jealousy, fear, had tried to rip them up, to eliminate the traces of their existence here. They had tried to dislodge the living, and even the dead. But human beings and cherry trees, even replanted far from their native soil, bring forth fruit that carries a memory of the fields that once nourished them.

In this fruit's red flesh, the blood of their ancestors howls.

The cherries of Westhoffen, just like its children, never really die. They can be preserved, even when they're plucked from their land. You only need to plunge them into *eau-de-vie* and they revive. And from generation to generation, this lively spirit has them repeating, "*L'Chaim!*"

Delphine Horvilleur is one of the few female rabbis in France. She was ordained in America, as there was no possibility to study in France as a woman, and is the leader of the Liberal Jewish Movement of France. Her writings have appeared in *The Washington Post* and *Haaretz*. She lives in Paris.